Hoos
IN THE KITCHEN

Recipes from the UVA Community

MASCOT BOOKS

HOOS

IN THE KITCHEN

Recipes from the UVA Community

Melissa Palombi

photos by
Sarah Cramer Shields

OFFICIALLY LICENSED PRODUCT

Immense Thanks

I am forever grateful to all the participants in this book, and thank you to a few who went above and beyond.

James King, thank you for generously hosting our potluck event on the beautiful property of King Family Vineyards. Your staff was friendly and easy to work with; they made the day an absolute pleasure.

MS Events, thank you for supplying the beautiful table decor for the photo shoot. It could not have happened without your unique resources.

Thank you to Nature Composed for providing beautiful flowers for this event, and to Gallatin Canyon for showing us your amazing talent.

I could not have done the King Family Vineyard photo shoot without the generous help of Kelsey Harrell. Kelsey assisted in planning this event, as well as setting the outstanding tablescape. Thank you for your day of event coordination with Karen Walker and the staff from The Catering Outfit.

Sarah Cramer Shields, you are my mentor and most enthusiastic cheerleader on this project. I admire your talent and never-ending positive energy in the way you engage with others. I hope this is the beginning of learning from you, and I hope we can work together again soon. Your photography makes this book come alive.

Thanks to Vanessa Larson, a talented editor and my friend for over twenty years who has helped in all my writing pursuits.

And most importantly, I thank my mother, who believes in doing what you are passionate about. She has supported this project in every way to make that happen.

-Melissa

Melissa and her mother, Phyllis

Contents

INTRO

For someone new to Charlottesville, this cookbook was an ambitious endeavor to get to know people associated with the University of Virginia. I love how food can tell a story. It is your history, where you came from, and what you want to share with others. Food is love, passion, history, and genuine curiosity. If you knew my family's culinary history, you would think the idea of me putting together a cookbook is no surprise. Growing up, holidays in my house were expressions of joy, with cooking together in the kitchen as a creation of memories. Food is an interesting way to get to know someone. What kind of food do they like to eat? What kind of restaurants do they prefer? What makes them nostalgic? This book is as much about the people in it as it is about the food.

One of my first assignments in the Athletics Department was to make sure the video crews producing each sporting event were fed. Although I wasn't the one cooking, I got to know vendors and caterers. Frank Smith, a caterer featured later in the book, helped spark the idea for *Hoos in the Kitchen*. The staff loves his food, and he and I got to know one another better by chatting about recipes. After learning how connected Frank is to UVA, I thought, *Why not get to know more about people who are connected with the University through food?*

This collection of recipes is just a small sample of staff and alumni who are passionate about food for fun, education, or professionally. Who knew there were free cooking classes once a week at UVA's international center? Or that there was a Jefferson-era fruitcake recipe recently discovered in the Pavilion X renovation? Or that our famous mascot, the Cavalier on horseback, likes to cook lasagna? That UVA alum Mitch Frank is a writer for *Wine Spectator* magazine? I've discovered many UVA connections to food, and this felt like the perfect opportunity to share this unique perspective on the impressive UVA community.

I don't consider myself the author of this book. Instead, I think of myself more like a *curator*. I have been humbled by the generosity of each person's time and interest in sharing their stories about food and their love for the University of Virginia. This was an amazing opportunity to see how open the people of UVA were in forming a community and getting to know one another, with their love of food a common thread.

James and Kelley King, who are UVA alumni, generously opened their vineyard on a beautiful October evening during the production of this publication. The contributors met as one at King Family Vineyards and had a potluck to share their dishes. Photographed by the wonderful Sarah Cramer Shields, the spirit of the evening encapsulated the same spirit of the book—love for UVA and the community it offers.

The evening also served as a fundraiser for the Local Food Hub, represented by UVA alumna Laura Brown, and the UVA Morven Kitchen Garden, represented by then-manager Emily Salle. Both Laura and Emily graciously contributed recipes to this collection as well. The Charlottesville band Gallatin Canyon played contemporary Virginia bluegrass music, as the attendees sipped King Family Roseland white wine. Luke Wilson and Zach Blatter are UVA alumni and the band is locally represented by Sam Hill Entertainment, an agency whose partners are Hank Wells (Comm '95) and Andy Jaspen (Comm '99), furthering the band's UVA connection.

There are images from this fantastic event throughout the book, and I hope this is the beginning of friendships yet to be discovered over a glass of Virginia wine and a recipe from this cookbook.

Go Hoos!

Breakfast

Apple season is an exciting time in Charlottesville, where orchards abound. One of the most popular orchards is Carter Mountain, which has a spectacular view of the city, beautiful sunsets, and over a dozen varieties of apples. In 2012, Carter Mountain Orchard was honored with the distinction of becoming a Century Farm by the Virginia Department of Agriculture. The title is given to those farms that have been in operation for at least 100 consecutive years.

The Chiles family owns Carter Mountain and runs Chiles Peach Orchard, where I got my peaches for another recipe in this book. Chiles' orchards are truly family-run businesses, and you can see three generations of Chiles working at any of their locations today.

On your way to Monticello, drive slowly to the peak. You will be greeted by open rows of beautiful apple trees, the iconic Carter Mountain red barn, and friendly staff. The activity of the day can be to pick your own Golden Delicious apples for this recipe. On Thursday evenings in the summer, they are open late for music, food (including cider donuts), wine tasting, and hard cider sampling.

Melissa's Oatmeal Pancakes

TOPPED WITH CARAMELIZED APPLES AND
TOASTED COCONUT FLAKES

(yields 2–6 pancakes, depending on size)

½ cup of rolled oats
1 cup of water
1 cup of buttermilk pancake mix
¼ cup of almond milk
1 tablespoon butter (increase as needed to grease pan)
1 tablespoon sugar
1 Golden Delicious apple per person
Syrup, for serving (optional)
Toasted coconut flakes, for sprinkling

This is a very simple recipe and done mostly by sight.

Begin by cooking rolled oats according to package instructions. The oats can be quick-cooking or not, whichever is preferred. While the oats are cooking, peel, core, and slice your apples. Then, melt butter in a pan on medium heat. Once heated, add apples and sugar. Sauté until golden, then set aside.

Prepare buttermilk pancake mix with almond milk according to package instructions. The almond milk will add a nutty flavor with the coconut later. Add cooked oats to buttermilk batter and add almond milk as needed. They should be thick but thinner than classic oatmeal.

In a skillet, fry pancakes until they have a golden underside, then flip. Plate pancakes as they come off the pan, add drips of syrup, and top with warmed apples and toasted coconut. I prefer Dang Toasted Coconut Flakes from Whole Foods because they are appropriately named.

Serve dishes one at a time, made to order. Eat 'em while they're hot!

Kelly Rossi

ASSISTANT DIRECTOR OF SPORTS NUTRITION

Kelly Rossi joined the Virginia Athletics Department in August 2011. With her passion for food, exercise, and culture, Charlottesville became the perfect place. The strong community connection with local famers also attracted Kelly to the city. She looks forward to Saturday mornings when she can walk the Charlottesville City market and feel the city's energy, while watching the farmers and craftspeople at work.

Working with busy student-athletes, it's important to help them find foods that not only support their performance but are also quick, tasty, and easy to prepare. Kelly's high-protein Peanut Butter Swirl Mason Jar Oatmeal does just the trick and more!

Kelly resides in Charlottesville with her husband, Reed, and dog, Bubba. She is living her dream and is grateful to be able to work with the staff and student athletes at such a wonderful school and in an amazing town.

High-Protein Swirl

VANILLA PEANUT BUTTER SWIRL MASON JAR OATMEAL

¼ cup rolled oats
2 tablespoons vanilla whey protein powder
1 tablespoon peanut butter
¼ cup 1 percent milk
¼–⅓ cup water

Place all dry ingredients in a mason jar. Add milk and water and shake vigorously. Refrigerate overnight.

The next morning, remove from refrigerator and shake vigorously. Remove lid and heat in microwave for intervals of 20–30 seconds. Stir regularly until shake reaches desired consistency.

Male athletes should double this recipe.

Bradley Kipp Darden '09

CO-OWNER OF RANDOM ROW BREWING COMPANY

Bradley Kipp moved to Charlottesville in 2007 at his wife's suggestion. As a UVA alumna, she loved the city and all it has to offer. After graduating from the Darden School of Business, Kipp began his entrepreneurial career in Charlottesville, too. With several technology start-ups and years of homebrewing under his belt, Bradley co-founded Random Row Brewing with Kevin McElroy.

Random Row is proud to be local. Everyone in the company has ties to Charlottesville—from its brewer all the way to individual investors.

In fact, even the name is a nod to Charlottesville's past. Random Row used to be the name of the brewery's neighborhood.

From IPAs to ales to stouts, Random Row is constantly experimenting with new recipes. Part of Bradley's job includes sampling new beers. It's a tough job, but someone has to do it. And this breakfast casserole is the perfect dish after a night of too many samples.

Morning After Breakfast Casserole

1½ pounds cooked ham, cubed
12 ounces sharp cheddar cheese, cubed
¾ pound loaf bread, cubed
8 large eggs
2 cups milk
1 cup cream
1 stick butter, melted
Tabasco, Worcestershire, and salt and pepper to taste

The night before, combine ham, cheese, and bread in a large bowl. In a separate bowl, beat eggs and add milk, cream, and butter. Add Tabasco, Worcestershire, and salt and pepper to taste. Mix wet ingredients into dry ingredients.

Grease a 9×13 casserole dish and pour in mixture. Refrigerate overnight.

The next day, preheat oven to 350°F. Bake the casserole uncovered for 60–90 minutes.

Top with Tabasco, and enjoy with a Random Row beer.

Hillary Lewis Darden '13

OWNER AND CREATOR OF LUMI JUICE

When Hillary Lewis first set foot on Darden's grounds, it immediately felt like home. The professors, students, and staff welcomed everyone with open arms, and there was a sense of community from the beginning.

After graduation, Hillary chose to stay in Charlottesville because of the wonderful qualities and traditions it offers. The festivals, charity runs, and farmers' markets are part of the Charlottesville experience, and Hillary takes them in whenever she can. She's also a fan of some of Charlottesville's favorite restaurants, like C&O, Tavola's Back Bar, Mas, and Boylan.

Inspired by her love of Charlottesville and healthy living, she created cold-pressed juice and founded Lumi Juice. It's her goal to help people build and maintain a well-balanced diet, and Charlottesville is just one of many communities her company helps. Lumi Juice also works with professional sports teams, like the Washington Wizards, Washington Nationals, and New York Yankees. And in keeping with community tradition, Lumi Juice even sources some of its fruits and veggies from local organic farmers!

Charlottesville offers so many exciting adventures. Where else can you get the culture of a big city with the benefits of the great outdoors? Hillary remains thankful every day to be able to live, work, and play here.

Lumi
Wahoo Power Shake

10 ounces Lumi Wahoo Orange
1 scoop vanilla protein powder
½ cup almond milk

Combine and enjoy!

Jason Becton & Patrick Evans

MarieBette Café & Bakery is a labor of love for Jason Becton and Patrick Evans. The two met in culinary school in New York City, which is also where their Charlottesville story begins.

Jason, a New Jersey native, left a career in advertising and worked in the kitchen at the Four Seasons Hotel for several years. Dedicated to his craft, he worked his way up from a line cook to a restaurant chef. Patrick, a fine artist and native of Albemarle County, worked at Michelin-starred restaurants Blue Hill New York City and Eighty-One before settling into baking. He honed his skills at Amy's Bread in New York City and then as the executive baker at Choc-O-Pain Bakery in New Jersey.

After starting a family, they decided to move to Albemarle County to start their own business. Named after their daughters Marian and Betty, MarieBette is a dream come true.

MarieBette's goal is to provide Charlottesville with breads, pastries, and savory menu items using local ingredients and artisanal techniques. The surrounding area of Albemarle County and beyond provides a rich source of vegetable, meat, and dairy options, all of which are featured on the menu. MarieBette serves breakfast, lunch, and baked goods seven days a week and is proud to be part of the Charlottesville community.

Lemon Ricotta Pancakes

(serves 8)

10 large eggs, separated
2 cups ricotta cheese
1 cup all-purpose flour
1 cup sugar
4 ounces (1 stick) of melted butter and an additional 2 tablespoons
    for the griddle pan
1½ teaspoons grated lemon zest
½ teaspoon kosher salt
Powdered sugar and maple syrup for garnish

In a large mixing bowl, combine egg yolks, ricotta, flour, sugar, melted butter, lemon zest, and salt. Whisk until smooth.

In the bowl of a stand mixer fitted with a whisk, whip the egg whites on high speed until they form stiff peaks. Using the whisk, gently stir in one quarter of the egg whites into the ricotta mixture until combined. Then pour in the rest of the egg whites and gently fold until combined.

Preheat an oven to 200°F to keep your finished pancakes warm during the process.

Heat a large skillet (nonstick or cast iron) or griddle over medium heat. Fold a sheet of paper towel in half and moisten with the rest of the melted butter. Carefully rub the skillet with the buttered paper towel.

Ladle the batter onto the griddle or into the skillet. Use the back of the ladle to spread and form the pancakes.

Cook until the surface of the pancake has bubbles, about 2 minutes. Flip carefully with a thin spatula, and cook until browned on the underside, about 1–2 minutes more. Be careful not to overcook and dry out the pancakes.

Transfer to a baking sheet or platter. Cover loosely with aluminum foil, and place in preheated oven to keep warm until all the pancakes are done.

Dust with powdered sugar and serve with real maple syrup.

Wendy Bolger Darden '01
& Anna Fife Darden '14

The University of Virginia's Darden School of Business is known for its committed and gregarious alumni network. The bond that students form on Grounds extends not only to their classmates but spans across generations of MBA graduates.

Wendy Bolger and Anna Fife share a connection to Darden as well as a passion for innovation and entrepreneurship in the social sector. That mutual interest led them both to Share Our Strength, an organization founded with the belief that everyone has strengths to share in the fight against hunger and poverty, and that solutions lie in these shared strengths. The organization is known for finding scalable, pragmatic solutions to social problems. Today, it is focused on ending child hunger in America, where one in five kids do not get the food they need, through the No Kid Hungry campaign.

A Charlottesville native, Anna Fife knew that she wanted to find a way to support strong food systems after spending a winter break in college working at Feast! Prior to Darden, she had the opportunity to work on agriculture policy for Virginia senator Mark Warner and gained an appreciation for the diversity of food grown and produced across the Commonwealth. She joined Share Our Strength after business school because of the unique intersection of food, public policy, and social impact. Her work gives her the opportunity to be part of the movement to ensure kids have the fuel they need to reach their full potential. And she loves being able to walk down the hall to collaborate and get advice from a fellow Darden grad.

Share Our Strength had been on Wendy's radar for years because of founders Billy and Debbie Shore's leadership as social entrepre-

neurs and their proven approach to ending childhood hunger through strategic partnership. Her work at the organization started when a classmate from Darden who was working at Share Our Strength brought her in on a consulting project. The projects grew, and in January 2016, she came on board full-time to lead the Program Innovation team. Wendy's team works to ensure that all kids who qualify can easily and conveniently access healthy meals at school and in the summer. Wendy loves doing this work with other Darden alums who have a shared language and a common understanding about expectations and management of a best-in-class organization.

As a mom, Wendy knows from experience what a difference a good breakfast makes in a kid's day. She loves to host friends at her house, and often finds that brunch is the best time of day to invite families with babies or young kids to accommodate nap schedules. Her go-to recipe is quiche; it's high-protein and easy to make ahead of time and customize according to dietary preferences or requirements. She swaps in dairy-free milk and manchego cheese made from sheep's milk for those intolerant to dairy, and kids' biases for broccoli or bell peppers over mushrooms, for example, can easily be accounted for. Wendy and Anna admitted to each other that they usually save a step by buying a premade crust (make it healthier by choosing a whole-grain crust). If you are feeling ambitious, a homemade savory pastry crust is definitely an upgrade!

Ham and Broccoli Quiche

(yields 9-inch quiche, serves 6)

1 9-inch packaged or homemade pie crust
½ cup broccoli florets, chopped
3 large eggs
1 cup of heavy cream
½ cup of whole or 2 percent milk
½ teaspoon salt
¼ teaspoon ground black pepper or cayenne pepper
Pinch of ground nutmeg (optional)
1 cup grated Gruyere or Swiss cheese
½ cup cooked ham, diced

Preheat oven to 375°F.

Place frozen or refrigerated premade pie crust in its tin onto a cookie sheet. If you're making your own crust, prepare and blind-bake a 9-inch pie crust.

Blanche the broccoli florets by adding them to a pot of boiling water for 60–90 seconds. Drain the broccoli in a colander and run under cold water. Set the broccoli aside to dry.

In a bowl, beat together eggs, heavy cream, milk, salt, pepper, and nutmeg (if using).

Spread the ham, broccoli, and grated cheese on the bottom of the pie shell. Pour egg mixture over ingredients in the pie shell. You may have some of the egg mixture left over.

Bake until the filling is solid in the center and slightly browned, about 40–50 minutes.

Slice and serve. It is best served warm with a side salad or fresh fruit.

Appetizers

Kate Collier Col '94

OWNER OF **FEAST!** (FEASTVIRGINIA.COM), AND FOUNDER OF THE LOCAL FOOD HUB (LOCALFOODHUB.ORG)

Carefully, lovingly produced food takes so much time and effort, it's hard to believe it can exist. How can the heirloom tomato farmer plant a seed, wait for it to sprout, transplant it in the field, trellis the plants so the tomatoes don't rot, pick the fruit, sort it for perfection, put it in a box, sell it, deliver it, and bill for it, all for just $2 per pound? In a world where making lots of money is a main driver for many, and cheap, easy food is an expectation of most, what is the future of specialty food? That is a question Kate Collier has been struggling with for years. She thinks it comes down to food appreciation, community connections, and engaging storytelling that will add value to food made with special care. The premise is if people care and know more about the food they put into their bodies, they will seek foods grown without chemicals and made with only good ingredients. They will pay the price that will keep family growers and producers in business into the future. It's a big, complex, worldwide problem, bringing in questions of industrialization, environmentalism, economics, politics, and science, so Kate focuses locally in Charlottesville.

Kate is a native Virginian. She grew up on a small farm in Fauquier County, where her family ran a wholesale shortbread cookie bakery and a seasonally inspired restaurant. Food—sourcing it, cooking it, and selling it—was their way of life. As a history major and sociology minor at UVA, she learned valuable skills in research, storytelling, and consumer analysis. These skills helped her land a job in San Francisco with a specialty food distributor, selling fine cheese and freshly cut salad greens to the Bay Area's most acclaimed restaurateurs.

In 2002, Kate Collier returned to Charlottesville and opened the specialty food store Feast! near Grounds. It quickly became a destination for Charlottesville's food lovers, who flocked to the bountiful cut-to-order cheese and cured meat counter and filled their baskets with local produce and wine. After two years, Feast! added a casual lunch café, where chefs take all the ingredients the store offers and cook them up into healthy, delicious soups, salads, and sandwiches.

Today, Feast! is the heart of Charlottesville's food scene. It is a bustling, warm, and welcoming place where students, tourists, and townspeople meet to enjoy food from sources they trust and are proud to support.

As the business grew, so did purchasing from local farmers and food producers. Through purchasing local produce, Kate heard a common concern. Farmers told her that they farmed because they enjoyed making their land productive. But they struggled with the business of sales, delivery, and billing. What they needed was a local food distributor. In 2009, with community support and funding, Kate started Local Food Hub, a nonprofit, local food distribution and farmer education service. Local Food Hub's sales and delivery services allow schools, hospitals, retailers, and restaurants to easily source and serve local food. It puts money (more than $3 million so far) back into Central Virginia's struggling rural economy and delivers fresher, healthier food to local families.

So what is Kate's favorite thing to cook? An antipasto platter, of course. It is fun to shop for and takes no actual cooking. Just go to your favorite specialty food store or farmers' market, and pick up all that looks delicious: ripe fruit, two or three cheeses, sliced salami, olives, tomatoes, crackers, crusty bread, and mustards. Pull out your platters or a cutting board, and have fun laying out the feast you selected. Open some wine or a beer, dig in, and enjoy discussing the variety of tastes.

Emily Salle Col '15

Emily Salle graduated from the College of Arts and Sciences in 2015 with a degree in environmental science. By this point, her primary interests were food production and experimental agriculture, but that hadn't always been the case.

After graduating high school, Emily deferred college admission to take a job teaching English in Spain. After spending seven months in Madrid, she ventured out of the city to work on small organic farms in the north. This led her to Galicia, Spain's northwestern autonomous region that abounds with verdant rolling hills, mossy forests, incredible coasts, and ancient monastery plantations of chestnut trees and grapevines. In Galicia, Emily spent two months working on family farms, learning methods of organic vegetable production as well as beekeeping and basic livestock management. At the end of those two months, she returned to the United States where, now thoroughly enchanted with agriculture, she spent the summer on a goat dairy farm just a few hours from her family's home in Richmond, Virginia. To Emily, producing good food has implied being in beautiful places with great, passionate people and using her entire being to work hard for something essential and wholesome.

These experiences taught her several things: how to understand the native Galician language, why seaweed is used to mulch tomatoes, and that small-scale, sustainable agriculture is key to navigating a future stricken with environmental degradation, overpopulation, and climate change.

In the fall of 2013, Emily became a volunteer at UVA's Morven Kitchen, which grows more than 2,000 pounds of these vegetables per year (and rising!) that are sold or donated to members of the community. The Morven Kitchen Garden quickly took on the exciting role of an agricultural observatory for Emily, playing out the narrative of her environmental science education in real time.

She later became the farm manager until 2016, providing support to the students who give the farm life. These students are from all years and come from all departments in the University and beyond. The farm also holds an annual event called Gazpacho in the Garden. Guests are asked to bring their own bowls and spoons, and students provide a dinner of homemade gazpacho, local breads, and an abundance of dishes featuring the tastes of summer. All are encouraged to bring family, friends, picnic blankets, chairs, and outdoor games as they dine outside in the Morven Kitchen Garden. It is a pay-what-you-can fundraiser for the UVA Morven Kitchen Garden. While she's no longer the farm manager, Emily still feels passionate about the farm's mission.

Gazpacho

(serves approximately 10)

7½ pounds ripe slicing tomatoes
2½ cucumbers
1 small red onion
4 cloves of garlic
1 cup of cilantro (½ of a large bunch)
3 ounces red wine vinegar
6 ounces olive oil
Salt and pepper to taste

Blanch and peel the tomatoes. Combine all ingredients in the order listed in a food processor. You may need to split into smaller batches to be able to process all the ingredients.

Chill for at least 12 hours before serving.

Watermelon and Tomato Gazpacho

2 cups seedless watermelon
2 pounds peeled ripe tomatoes
½ seedless cucumber, peeled and coarsely chopped
½ small red onion, coarsely chopped
1 small red bell pepper, seeded and coarsely chopped
½ jalapeño, chopped
Juice of 1 lime
Handful of chopped flat-leaf parsley
Salt and pepper to taste

Garnish

Cubed avocado
Chopped red onion
Olive oil

Combine all ingredients in a food processor and blend. Season to taste. Garnish with splash of avocado, red onion, and olive oil.

Robin VanHall, RD

OUTPATIENT REGISTERED DIETITIAN AT UVA'S
NORTHRIDGE NUTRITION COUNSELING CENTER

Robin VanHall has been at UVA in different capacities since 2005. She appreciates each one but has landed in her ideal position doing outpatient nutrition counseling. She is overflowing with gratitude for getting to know people ranging from academics to those from the medical center. She is delighted to be at the hub of where the two sides of UVA meet to explore the journey to wellness. Her goal is to create a safe and comforting space that allows creativity to flow from each individual she encounters. Her objective is to explore wellness intricately and collaborate with people to help everyone find self-empowerment to achieve their goals.

Robin prides herself on her active listening to get the whole picture. Putting people's thoughts and feelings into action is her goal. Food is something we all absolutely need. How we get there is the only difference, and there is not one way better than another, only the one that is created individually. She believes we all need a daily dose of laughter to stay nourished and that we can all create a swirl of wellness across the community. Those who are struggling can hitch a ride with those who are already rolling along on this will-to-be-healthy journey.

Going into nutrition was a natural fit for her, as she grew up loving every sport possible. A soccer injury, however, led her to the love of running. But even now, despite rain, snow, sleet, or heat, you will find her outdoors whenever possible. She attributes this to growing up with the seasonal varieties of Michigan. She relishes the memories of always having lakes nearby to jump in and now cherishes climbing the beautiful mountains here in Virginia.

Robin encourages everyone to take time out to explore wellness.

Her Caprese Skewers with Balsamic Drizzle are perfect bites of freshness. Enjoy this healthy appetizer recipe year-round.

Caprese Skewers with Balsamic Drizzle

1 cup balsamic vinegar
Cherry or grape tomatoes
Mini mozzarella cheese balls (could use a regular-
    sized ball cut into bite-sized pieces)
Fresh basil leaves
Salt and pepper to taste

Bring balsamic vinegar to a boil in a small saucepan. Then lower heat to medium and simmer until it's the consistency of very thin maple syrup (about 10 minutes).

Pour into a bowl and let cool.

Cut tomatoes in half. Thread a mini mozzarella cheese ball, basil leaf (fold in half if large), and a tomato half onto a toothpick. Repeat with remaining ingredients.

Sprinkle with salt and pepper. Drizzle cooled balsamic reduction on top.

Note: You can serve the tomato, mozzarella, and basil if you do not like or have time for the drizzle.

Emma Terry

PROGRAMS & COMMUNICATIONS MANAGER FOR UVA ARTS

Emma Terry likes to say she was born into the arts. Her mother was an amazing artist with a vibrant Carytown co-op gallery in Richmond, Virginia, called But is it Art? Her father is an extraordinary photographer and writer. Growing up in a household that celebrated experimentation and creativity from the start, Emma became an artist in her own right. She inherited her mother's love for studio art, building and sewing multimedia sculptures, and studying graphic design. And as her father's daughter, creative writing became an integral part of her daily routine by age six.

After graduating from William and Mary, and despite her childhood, Emma found herself accidentally working in finance for seven years. Disheartened and seeking a respite from work that was "stealing her soul," she took a year off to study ethnography and folklore at the University College Cork, Ireland. There, she learned the value of slow living and walking among the sheep on the rolling hills. She started to think it was time for a major change in her life.

In 2010, she decided to leave Richmond for Charlottesville with the goal of working for the University of Virginia in the arts. A few months and two interviews later, she became the staff assistant to the Vice Provost of the Arts in the Office of the Executive Vice President and Provost.

The past six years spent working at a world-class university have been incredibly fulfilling for Emma. As a young woman, she plotted how to become a lifelong professional student. Now tasked with collaborating with progressive thinkers to facilitate open forums for discourse, exhibition, and performance, working at UVA Arts gets her pretty close to that dream—and with a salary instead of tuition!

Emma's recipe is a product of her creative upbringing and the risk-taking and experimental mindset that led her from Carytown to County Cork to Charlottesville. This artistic attitude continues to inform much of her life, including cooking. For Emma, sharing a meal can be a great convener and a true culinary art when creativity is the secret ingredient. In the kitchen, she puts her imagination to work in serving unique and tasty dishes that bring people together to share something wonderful, memorable, and (fingers crossed) edible.

Black Bean Bowls were conceived by Emma's love of finger foods—most likely inspired by countless viewings of *Mermaids* with her sister—and Mexican cuisine. She combined her favorites into a bite-sized morsel of pure goodness, which is now a major headliner requested at every potluck she attends. Despite their miniature size, Emma likes to think this dish brings hefty, family-sized portions of joy to those around her. She will be forever happy to make them for all!

Black Bean Bowls

1 can (15 ounces) black beans, drained and rinsed
½ red bell pepper, diced
1 tomato, diced
1 small onion, diced
2 jalapeños, diced
8 ounces grated cheddar cheese
Salt and pepper to taste
50 square wonton wrappers

Preheat oven to 375°F. Combine all the ingredients except the wonton wrappers and cheese.

Spray a mini-muffin pan with oil. Fold in the wonton wrappers. Add a spoonful of filling and top with cheese. Fold/scrunch down edges of the wontons.

Bake for 7–8 minutes, until cheese is melted and wontons are golden brown. Best served with guacamole, salsa, and sour cream!

Dean Allan Groves Law '90

Dean Allan Groves feels fortunate to call himself an alumnus of the University, having graduated in 1990 from the School of Law. He spent the next sixteen years practicing law in a large Atlanta firm. However, for the past nine years, he has served as the University's Dean of Students, his dream job.

Essentially, this means he leads a team of people who work to create the best possible "outside the classroom" experience for UVA's undergraduate, graduate, and professional school students. Important aspects of his work include residential living communities on Grounds; over 600 student organizations, including fraternities and sororities, club sports, and political, religious, artistic, and cultural groups; student-gathering spaces across Grounds, including Newcomb Hall, Ern Commons, and the new Lloyd Building project on the Corner. Most critically, he is responsible for helping create a welcoming, inclusive, and safe environment for all students.

A wonderful aspect of his job is the daily contact he has with students. This includes annual dinners at his home with student members of the Raven Society, part of a program to connect faculty and student Ravens with each other in true Jeffersonian tradition. A favorite dish he serves at the start of the evening is bruschetta, an Italian classic. It's the perfect finger food to help facilitate pre-dinner conversation. Here is the Dean's version of it.

Bruschetta

3 cups cherry tomatoes
2 cups olive oil
3 sprigs thyme
3 sprigs rosemary
1 head of garlic
1 French baguette
Salt and pepper to taste
Parmesan cheese (optional)

Preheat oven to 400°F.

Combine all the above, except for salt and pepper and Parmesan cheese. Roast for 20–25 minutes, until bubbly.

Cut a large French baguette into ¼- to ½-inch slices. Lightly toast.

Place a generous portion of the cherry tomato mixture on the bread slices, making sure to spread out the tomatoes. You may need to remove the tomatoes from the olive oil mix and mash them up a bit first.

Add some of the olive oil mixture on top of the tomatoes and then finish with salt and pepper to taste. If desired, you can add freshly shaved Parmesan cheese before serving.

Pair with a hearty Virginia red wine.

Enrico Cesaretti Grad '91

DIRECTOR OF ITALIAN UNDERGRADUATE PROGRAMS

When Enrico Cesaretti left his native Tuscany more than twenty years ago to continue his graduate studies at the UVA Department of Spanish, Italian, and Portuguese, both the culinary scene and food choices in Charlottesville were very different from what he knew. Although he wasn't a picky eater, he remembers craving the just-out-of-the-oven warm, crusty bread and simple al dente pasta he used to have at home, or looking at usually misspelled restaurant menus that listed "Italian" dishes he had never heard of, such as fettuccine alfredo, chicken piccata, and shrimp scampi.

The realization that there seemed to be a very limited knowledge of what "real" Italian food was and the often stereotypical and inaccurate perception of the country it was associated with led him to appreciate the profound cultural value and communicative power of food.

In turn, it eventually encouraged him to reflect on the subject from a more scholarly perspective. The result was a series of essays that were situated at the junction of literary criticism and food studies. They eventually generated a book, *Fictions of Appetite: Alimentary Discourses in Italian Modernist Literature* (2013). This publication discusses the symbolic power and aesthetic significance of images of food and eating (or not eating) in a selection of Italian novels, short stories, poems, essays, and plays written in the first four decades of the twentieth century, a period in which questions of alimentation often revealed latent tensions between private and public bodies and related to issues of gender, identity, and consumption. More recently, Enrico became especially interested in the central role food plays in local as well as global discourses about health, ecology, and sustainability, and how it crucially connects human and nonhuman natures.

As Director of Undergraduate Programs, he has also been very glad to support and integrate Dolcissimo: Speak the Sweet Life, a student dessert cooking competition, into the Italian Studies course curriculum. The following recipe, however, is not for a dessert but for Ribollita, a traditional Tuscan bean and cabbage soup that was a typical peasants' dish. Nowadays, it appears on the menus of upscale restaurants from New York City to San Francisco.

Ribollita

(serves 4)

½ cup extra-virgin olive oil
1 medium red onion, chopped into ½-inch dice
2 cloves garlic, peeled and thinly sliced
1 medium carrot, scraped and chopped into ¼-inch half-moons
2 ribs celery, chopped into ¼-inch thick pieces
2 waxy potatoes, peeled and cut into ½-inch cubes
3 cups cannellini or borlotti beans, soaked and cooked (canned are fine, too)
6 cups reserved bean liquid (or water)
1 cup basic tomato sauce
1 bunch Swiss chard, chopped into ½-inch ribbons
1 bunch kale, chopped into ½-inch ribbons
1 bunch black cabbage (cavolo nero), chopped into ½-inch ribbons
4 slices country bread, toasted
½ cup grated Parmigiano

The night before, heat the oil in an 8-quart pot. Add the onion and garlic, and cook until soft. Add carrots, celery, potatoes, 2 cups of beans, bean cooking liquid (or water), and basic tomato sauce, and bring to a boil.

Lower heat, add chard, kale, black cabbage, and simmer 1½ hours, or until everything is soft. Add the remaining beans and adjust seasonings.

Allow to cool and rest overnight.

The following day, bring to a boil. Serve in shallow bowls over toasted bread. Sprinkle with Parmigiano tableside.

Ashley Matthews Law '12 & Dave Koehn
"Voice of the Virginia Cavaliers"

Dave Koehn and Ashley Matthews met in Texas, when Dave was the play-by-play voice of Texas Lutheran University and Ashley was home from NYU's School of Journalism, writing for the local newspaper.

Dave's career finally took them to Charlottesville, where he became the "Voice of the Virginia Cavaliers." And while Dave gave the play-by-plays at UVA's sporting events, Ashley attended the School of Law and received her J.D. from the University in 2012.

Ashley admits that she was pretty oblivious to sports before she met Dave, but they love how the UVA sports community focuses on both academics and character. It's really fun—and easy—to cheer for the good men and women.

In addition to sports, when Ashley can tag along with Dave to games at other ACC schools, they spend a lot of time finding great restaurants. Dave often tweets a restaurant pick for each road trip, but they have some repeat favorites too.

In Charlottesville, they love to eat at The Shebeen, Brazos Tacos, and Peter Chang's China Bistro. A favorite hidden gem is Café 88; it's Charlottesville's best-kept secret! If you decide to visit, make sure to try the scallion pancakes and the fried tofu bento box.

Dave serves on the board of directors for Big Brothers and Big Sisters of the Central Blue Ridge, and they've both served on the Bowl for Kids' Sake committee for four years.

Before living in Charlottesville, Dave and Ashley lived in Vermont and took frequent visits to Montreal and Quebec City, where they searched tirelessly for the perfect bowl of French onion soup. This recipe, now with a few of Ashley's tweaks, is the first "fancy" recipe she learned to cook. It's still her go-to when they have something to celebrate. The result is well worth the time it takes to caramelize the onions!

Photo Credit:
Matt Riley

"Fancy" French Onion Soup

4 tablespoons butter
1 teaspoon salt
2 large red onions, thinly sliced
2 large Vidalia onions, thinly sliced
2 cans (14 ounces) low-sodium beef broth
2 cans (14 ounces) low-sodium chicken broth
½ cup red wine
1 tablespoon Worcestershire sauce
2 sprigs fresh parsley
1 sprig fresh thyme
1 bay leaf
1 tablespoon balsamic vinegar
4 thick slices French or Italian bread
4–8 slices Swiss cheese
½ cup shredded mozzarella cheese
Salt and pepper to taste
Dash of paprika (optional)

In a large pot, melt butter over medium-high heat. Stir in salt and pepper to taste, red onions, and Vidalia onions. Cook at least 35 minutes, stirring frequently, until onions are caramelized.

Add chicken broth, beef broth, red wine, and Worcestershire sauce.

Use twine to create a bouquet garni with the parsley, thyme, and bay leaf and add to the pot. Simmer 20 minutes over medium heat, stirring occasionally.

Remove and discard the herbs, reduce to low heat, and stir in vinegar and salt and pepper to taste.

Toast or broil bread slices until toasted and firm.

Fill oven-safe bowls half to three-quarters full of the soup, top each with a bread slice, and layer on 1 or 2 slices of Swiss cheese and a handful of the shredded mozzarella. Top with a sprinkle of paprika if desired. Broil 2–3 minutes, until the cheese is bubbling and toasted.

Frank Smith Col '86

UNCLE FRANK'S CATERING

When asked about his gastronomical background, Frank Smith of Uncle Frank's Catering can weave a fanciful tale, one every bit as rich as the soups, jambalaya, barbecue, and gumbo he serves the UVA Athletic Department's video crew on game days.

"Well," he'll drawl, "there were those years spent on the old Chisolm Trail during cattle drives. There's nothing like campfire cooking under open skies for a mess of hungry cowpokes. I can still hear the bell clang when I'd call 'em in for supper." He pauses. "But then, that time spent in northern France—learning *l'art boulanger*, all those apprenticeships at the Michelin restaurants—that left a few *souvenance chaleureuse,* too. And there was the shrimping in New Orleans...a summer in Jamaica, perfecting the Blue Mountain brew technique... one amazing month in South Carolina, exploring the deep and subtle nuances of redeye gravy. Oh, there were lots of things."

Closer inspection, however, reveals a grin, and Frank's tongue firmly planted in cheek. His actual culinary background is a lot less cinematic. Two aunts, both amazing cooks, awakened his interest in cooking when he was in high school. When he arrived at the University of Virginia in the late '70s, those seeds began to flower and take root. Lessons were learned (and not a few laughs had) as he experimented with friends who honed their kitchen skills through trial and error, all seeking the prize of home-cooked food at day's end. This paid dividends after graduation, when he married his wife, Judy, and headed to Gordon-Conwell Theological Seminary (GCTS). While Judy paid the bills as a nurse, Frank returned home after studies and made the meals.

It was at GCTS that he was exposed to a variety of cultural and international influences as students and professors came from all over the world. Over time, Frank learned the history and use of spices, the differences between grilling and smoking, and the arts of slow cooking, sauce making, and even coffee roasting. He was additionally blessed to have a variety of dinner guests who enjoyed cooking and would graciously taste his attempts and then share their own techniques and experiences.

Six years in campus ministry at Michigan State University followed, during which cooking was put on a back shelf. But when Frank, Judy, and their two children moved back to Charlottesville in 1997, he decided to return to the kitchen and start up the smoker. Uncle Frank's Catering was born, the name arising from the many "nephews and nieces" of friends, and Frank now cooks for weddings, corporate events, and holiday parties—as well as annual reunions with those best friends made in the glory days of Jeff Lamp and Ralph Sampson. All members of the Fellowship of Christian Athletes (FCA), they went to every basketball game they could and every stop on Virginia's way to the 1981 Final Four. And now, they're looking forward to repeating that experience one day soon!

Butternut Squash Soup

2 tablespoons butter
½ cup coarsely chopped onion
4 tablespoons flour
3 cups chicken stock
1 cup vegetable stock
3 large butternut squash, peeled,
    seeded, and cut into 1-inch cubes
¼ cup light brown sugar
1 teaspoon cayenne pepper
1 cup heavy cream
Salt to taste (not much)

Heat butter in a saucepan. Add the onion, and cook until wilted. Sprinkle in the flour, stirring to mix. When the flour is blended well into the butter and onion, add the stocks, stirring rapidly with a whisk till smooth.

Add the squash, and simmer about 40 minutes. Stir occasionally to keep it from sticking. When the squash is quite tender, use the whisk and chop it into little bits in the soup.

Using blender (two batches) purée the soup and then return to saucepan. Add brown sugar, more or less to taste; we like a sweeter soup. Then add the cayenne and just a bit of salt. Add the cream, and bring just to the boil, stirring the whole time. Serve hot.

There's lots of stirring with a flour and cream soup, but the velvety smooth taste at the end says, "Well worth it!"

Salads & Sides

Tommy Viar Engr '73

Tommy Viar is an avid home cook and recommends these recipes as time-tested and worthy UVA football tailgate options. He has a huge affinity for UVA sports, as he was born in Charlottesville, attended Albemarle High School, and played football for UVA from 1968 to 1972. He received his B.S. in nuclear engineering in 1973, the first football player at the University to do so.

Tommy calls himself a dyed-in-the-wool Wahoo! His father, William L. Viar, attended UVA, lettered in boxing, and earned his B.S. degree in mechanical engineering in 1952. He also severed as president of the University's School of Engineering and Applied Science after teaching from 1962 to 1974. In fact, Tommy even had his father as a professor for three classes, but he received no slack.

Tommy's wife, Jody Harris, works for the Virginia Athletics Foundation and is his "bestest tailgate buddy." They live in what they call their "piece of Heaven," named North Garden, which is south of Charlottesville.

Bok Choy Salad

2 pounds bok choy
10 scallions (green onions)
4 tablespoons butter
5 ounces sliced almonds
¼ cup sesame seeds
2 packages ramen noodles (broken up)
½ cup oil
½ cup sugar (substitute with stevia, if preferred)
⅛ cup white vinegar
3 tablespoons soy sauce

Chop bok choy and scallions, using both the green and white parts. Place in a bowl.

In a large frying pan, melt butter and sauté almonds, sesame seeds, and ramen noodles until brown. Do not over-toast sesame seeds and almonds. Toasting is designed to release oils in the seeds and nuts. Burning them will yield a burnt taste. Set aside to cool.

In a separate bowl, mix oil, sugar, vinegar, and soy sauce for the dressing.

When you are ready to serve, mix the almonds, sesame seeds, and noodle mixture with the bok choy and scallions. Give the dressing a good whisk, and add the desired amount. Mix well and serve.

Frank Smith's
Green Goddess Dressing

6 scallions (green onions)
½ cup honey
½ cup white sugar
2 teaspoons salt
2 teaspoons white pepper
⅔ cup rice wine vinegar
1⅓ cups peanut oil

Chop scallions coarsely and put into a blender. Follow with honey, sugar, salt, white pepper, and rice wine vinegar. Begin blending.

After a minute, while continuing to blend, pour the peanut oil in a thin steam into the center of the blender (the "eye" of the dressing hurricane, so to speak). If the dressing seems a little thick, add 1 or 2 tablespoons of water.

This dressing tastes absolutely fantastic and is especially good on salads that incorporate fresh fruit, such as strawberries and mandarin oranges, alongside the lettuce. Its background is Asian sweet and sour. As there are no gums or artificial emulsifiers, the dressing will separate after a few hours, but a quick shake will put it to rights.

Liz Wellbeloved-Stone Col '87

ASSISTANT DIRECTOR OF UVA IN VALENCIA

Liz Wellbeloved-Stone has worked as the assistant director of the UVA in Valencia, Spain, program since May 2000. The program, which began in 1983, is the flagship study abroad program at UVA, featuring courses in Spanish literature, culture, history, art, and language. Since its inception, there have been over 8,000 participants from UVA and dozens of other institutions across the United States.

Liz graduated from Charlottesville High School in 1983 and received a B.A. in Spanish from UVA in 1987, after studying abroad in Valencia for one year. Her two children, James (Col '12) and Claire, were the first second-generation students to enroll in the Valencia program.

Valencia is famous for its rice, and paella is the crown jewel of Valencian cooking. Valencian paella contains green and white beans, chicken, rabbit, and snails. Seafood paella replaces the meat and vegetables with a wide range of fresh seafood, including mussels, shrimp, and cuttlefish. There are also mixed paellas that combine any assortment of ingredients. Each family has its own favorite recipe, often cooked outdoors over an open fire of pine and orange branches.

This version does not require a paella pan or an open flame but still evokes memories of sitting at a seaside restaurant, looking out at the Mediterranean, and sharing a lazy meal with friends and family.

Paella-Inspired Vegetarian Rice

Olive oil
1 cup chopped onion
½ cup chopped green bell pepper
3 cloves garlic, crushed
¼ teaspoon smoked paprika
Pinch of saffron strands
1½ cups paella rice (bomba if available; if not,
    substitute with arborio)
5 cups vegetable stock
1 cup frozen peas
1 cup frozen or fresh green beans, cut into
    approximately 1-inch pieces
1 cup chopped carrot
1 cup asparagus, cut into approximately 1-inch pieces
½ cup cauliflower florets
2 cups frozen artichoke heart halves
Salt and pepper to taste

Coat the bottom of a large pot with olive oil. Sauté onion, bell pepper, and garlic until softened. Add paprika and saffron. Stir in rice until it is coated with oil. Add stock and vegetables.

Bring to a boil, reduce heat, cover, and simmer until rice is tender, about 20 minutes. Check midway to be sure there is enough liquid. Add more stock as needed. Salt and pepper to taste.

Serve with a slice of lemon and garlic mayonnaise. Other vegetables can be added, such as lima beans, fava beans, red bell pepper, zucchini, or yellow squash. Part of the stock can be replaced by crushed tomatoes.

Willis Jenkins

ASSOCIATE PROFESSOR OF RELIGIOUS STUDIES

Willis Jenkins is an associate professor in the Religious Studies department. The author of two award-winning books on religion and environmental problems, Willis came to UVA as part of an environmental humanities initiative and teaches courses on the cultural dimensions of environmental issues. One of those courses is called the Moral Ecology of Food, which explores the entanglement of personal, political, ecological, and religious questions with food practices.

Willis grew up in rural Madison County, Virginia, and often worked on his grandparents' farm at the base of Old Rag Mountain. His grandmother cooked traditional Appalachian "holler" food, including bitter greens that simmered in fatback—home-cured from forest-ranged hogs—and served with sliced garden tomatoes. To Willis, the combination of those greens with the sweet acidity of the tomatoes tasted like the farm work itself: hot, bitter, smoky, and unendingly satisfying.

Later in life, he wanted to share that memory with family and friends, but without the pork, which now often comes from inhumane warehouses. After many experiments, he figured out that he needed to maintain the texture of the greens, work with their earthiness to bring out a robust umami flavor riding on their native bitterness, make them pop with acidity from vinegars, and add enough salt to bring out the flavor profile, with a note of spicy heat.

There are a number of ways to get there, and you can adapt the following recipe based on the kinds of greens you have and the ingredients at hand. Here's how he does it.

Braised Greens

Greens
Olive oil
6 cloves minced garlic (more or less; to your preference)
Dash of cayenne pepper
Diced tomatoes
3 cups strong vegetable broth
¼ cup vinegar (balsamic or white wine vinegar, but apple
    cider vinegar is traditional)
Lemon juice
Salt to taste

Start with a mess of greens—about how much would fit packed down into a large grocery bag—but almost any amount will do.

These greens can be of several kinds, including collards, mustard, kale, turnip, cress, chard, and beet. Willis' preference is a mix of collards (for texture) and purple mustard (for spiciness).

Remove ribs (aka stems), and rinse the leaves.

Blanch the greens for 2 minutes in boiling water, then rinse with cold water. This helps reduce the bitterness. The cold-water shock stops the cooking and helps maintain texture and color. If your greens are very young and tender, you can skip this step.

Put the greens (now reduced in size) on a cutting board, pack together tightly, and roughly chop.

In a large cast-iron skillet, slowly sauté minced garlic in olive oil along with a couple dashes of cayenne pepper. Add garlic and cayenne to taste.

Just as the garlic begins to turn golden, add diced tomatoes to cover the bottom of the skillet. Sauté tomatoes for a few minutes, making sure the garlic does not brown. Add the greens to skillet with a few more tablespoons of olive oil. Keep the heat low, letting it cook down a bit. Stir together to mix with the tomatoes and garlic.

Add vegetable broth to cover the bottom of the skillet about a half-inch deep (about 3 cups for a large skillet).

Let simmer uncovered on medium heat, stirring consistently. After about 20 minutes, the greens should have turned tender and dark green, and the tomatoes should have mostly cooked into liquid. If not, let simmer a while longer. If the greens seem well cooked but remain clumpy, add more olive oil.

Lower heat and add vinegar. Start with ¼ cup, stir, let it sit for a minute, and then taste. Keep adding vinegar until it is a distinctive element of the flavor profile.

Cover, and keep on very low simmer for 5 minutes (or turn off the heat and keep covered if serving later). Before serving, taste again for saltiness and acidity. Add a few drops of olive oil and lemon juice right before serving.

Willis' family sometimes makes a dinner of braised greens with polenta or grits and fried eggs. It feels perfect when made from ground Virginia cornmeal and eggs from their backyard hens.

Main Dishes

The following three recipes have been standards in my repertoire for dinner parties and groups of friends. You can make the ravioli in advance and freeze them to then be taken out and boiled in no time. The sage butter sauce for the butternut squash ravioli is made in minutes, and the lamb ragù can be made a day or two in advance, making life easy while making something impressive from scratch. To me, all are considered comfort foods, and Charlottesville shops source ingredients for fresh pasta and meat, taking the flavors to another level.

Mona Lisa Pasta on Preston Ave. allows me to continue to make my ravioli in Charlottesville. As lovely as it is to make pasta from scratch, it takes time and space to lay out the dough, so when you just want to make some fresh ravioli for the freezer, Mona Lisa Pasta has fresh pasta sheets ready for purchase by the pound. They have many flavors to choose from, including the rare squid ink pasta, which makes a solid black for when you want to serve the butternut squash ravioli for Halloween. They look great, with one side black squid ink, one side egg pasta, and orange butternut in the middle. In addition to fresh pasta of all shapes, Mona Lisa carries a large selection of premade ravioli, sauces, pizzas, sandwiches, and Italian products.

For the Pea and Mint Ravioli recipe, I use Mona Lisa Pasta's plain egg pasta sheets to let the fresh flavors stand on their own to pair with the lamb ragù. The ground lamb, Italian sausage, and pancetta from **JM Stock Provisions** elevate these recipes with a depth of flavor from their quality products.

JM Stock Provisions is a whole-animal butcher, working exclusively with local farms that produce grass-fed, pasture-raised animals. JM Stock founders James Lum and Matthew Greene launched the store to act as a retail location for local farmers, giving consumers more direct access to locally raised organic meats. This is the place for sausage.

On their website, www.jmstockprovisions.com, they have a list that tells you what is featured that week and, specifically, a sausage schedule. Some of their sausage varieties include Sweet Serrano, Chicken and Waffles, Banh Mi, and Pizza Party. For the recipe in this book, we'll stick with a classic sweet Italian sausage, which they also carry, but how fun to try new sausages!

On their website, JM Stock Provisions states, "We're the guys who believe responsibly produced food shouldn't just be accessible, it should be approachable. Our passion lies in creating a community of educated consumers, and reminding them that good food is for everyone." They live up to this credo, and when you walk into JM Stock Provisions, you experience not only great customer service but a partnership with the staff to help you find what you are looking for. It is a creative experience. You might have an idea of what you want, but they can help you achieve it and even give you cooking directions to prepare the meat you are about to purchase.

I had never made a dry-aged sirloin but took it upon myself to make it for the holidays for family and guests. I followed Matt Greene's suggestions carefully on seasoning, cooking time, and temperature, and the roast came out perfectly while being effortless.

JM Stock Provisions will make you look good and feel confident! If you really get hooked, they also offer butchery classes.

Butternut Squash Ravioli

in Sage Brown Butter Sauce

This butternut squash recipe is inspired from a traditional northern Italian recipe, specifically the city of Mantova (Mantua). The recipe dates back to the Renaissance, when it was served to Queen Christina of Sweden when she visited the region in Italy. Thomas Jefferson had an affinity for kitchen gadgets, like a pasta maker, and according to his personal library collection at the Library of Congress, there are manifestos from Queen Christina (two from 1636 and one from 1649). So while it is certainly quite the historical leap, I like to imagine perhaps Jefferson tasted a version of butternut squash ravioli similar to this.

What sets this butternut squash recipe apart from others are the sweet and spicy flavors created by a regional ingredient. Mostarda di Mantova adds a sweet (pear) and spicy (horseradish) flavor that cannot be recreated easily. If you cannot find it in specialty stores, it can be ordered online. This element keeps the ravioli special but does require some preplanning.

1 butternut squash (2 pounds), seeded and cut into chunks
    (substitute with orange-fleshed sweet potatoes)
2 cups freshly grated Parmigiano-Reggiano
1/3 cup apple or pear mostarda (preferably Mantovana),
    coarsely chopped
6 amaretti (Italian almond cookies), finely ground
1 teaspoon fresh lemon juice
1/8 teaspoon freshly grated nutmeg
Salt and freshly ground black pepper to taste
1/2 cup unsalted butter
2 tablespoons chopped sage

Preheat oven to 450°F. Line a baking pan with parchment paper; lightly oil. Place squash chunks on pan and bake until tender, 35–45 minutes. Remove from oven, and let cool for about 10 minutes. Remove and discard skin.

Scoop out flesh of squash into a bowl. Add 1½ cups cheese, mostarda, amaretti crumbs, lemon juice, and nutmeg. Season with salt and pepper to taste. Stir to combine well. Set aside.

Take out premade ravioli from Mona Lisa Pasta (or make your own). Roll the dough as thinly as possible. Put out one sheet to be the bottom of the ravioli. Put scant teaspoons of filling 1 inch from edge of dough, 2 inches apart. Gently place second rolled pasta sheet on top. Press around filling, so you can see where to cut.

Using a fluted pastry wheel, trim between mounds of stuffing to form squares. Dip a finger into cold water, then press down edges of squares to seal. Spread squares onto clean, dry dish towels.

If freezing for later use, place ravioli on a cookie sheet covered with plastic wrap or parchment, making sure they do not touch. Freeze overnight. The next day, remove from cookie sheet and put into a food storage bag or container before returning to the freezer. This ensures the ravioli will not stick together.

When ready to cook, bring a large pot of water to a boil. In a small saucepan, melt butter over medium-low heat. Stir in chopped sage and a generous pinch of salt. Reduce heat to low to keep warm.

Once cooking water is boiling, add salt and the ravioli. Cook until tender and all ravioli float to the top, about 4 minutes. Using a slotted spoon, transfer ravioli to pan and mix with sage butter.

Plate ravioli and sprinkle with cheese. Garnish with remainder of sage.

Pea & Mint Ravioli with Lamb Ragù

Ravioli

3 tablespoons olive oil
1 shallot, finely chopped (about ¼ cup)
1 garlic clove, minced
2¼ cups shelled fresh or thawed frozen peas
¼ cup plus 2 tablespoons dry white wine
1 cup water
Coarse salt and freshly ground pepper
1 tablespoon fresh mint leaves chopped, plus a few
    small leaves for garnish
3 tablespoons mascarpone cheese
Freshly grated Parmigiano-Reggiano to taste
½ teaspoon kosher salt

Lamb Ragù

3 tablespoons olive oil
1 onion, ¼-inch dice
1 carrot, finely chopped
1 celery rib, finely chopped
4 ounces or 2 ¼-inch slices of pancetta, diced into small chunks
1 teaspoon hot chili flakes
1½ pounds of ground lamb
1 cup dry red wine
1 tablespoon tomato paste
2 cans (15 ounces) chopped tomatoes
Kosher salt and freshly ground pepper
Freshly grated Pecorino Romano cheese to serve

Heat oil in a medium skillet over medium heat. Add shallot. Cook, stirring occasionally for 3–4 minutes, until translucent. Add garlic, cooking 2–3 minutes until soft.

Add peas, wine, 1 cup water, and 1½ teaspoons salt; season with pepper. Simmer until liquid has almost evaporated and peas are tender, 12–15 minutes. Add mint leaves after 10 minutes to warm through. Let cool slightly.

Place the pea mixture in a food processor. Add mascarpone and Parmesan cheese while mixture is still warm, and pulse to combine. Taste, and adjust seasoning to your preference.

Repeat step 2 from the Butternut Squash Ravioli recipe to create ravioli. Either freeze ravioli for a later date or boil water, add salt, and cook the ravioli.

While water is going to boil, you can start the ragù.

In a 10- to 12-inch, deep sauté pan, heat the olive oil over medium heat. Add the onion, carrot, and celery rib. Sweat until translucent and vegetables are just beginning to brown. Add the pancetta and chili flakes. Cook until the pancetta has rendered its fat.

Add ground lamb to the pan, and cook until done. Then, add the wine and simmer for 5 minutes. Add tomatoes, bring to a boil, then lower heat to a simmer and season with salt and pepper. Cover, and simmer gently until tomatoes reduce, about 20 minutes,

While the ragù simmers, cook your ravioli. Drain, but do not rinse.

Note: Do not leave ravioli in strainer! They will stick together. Add a little olive oil if needed to keep them separate.

Plate the ravioli either family style on a large platter or on small, individual plates. Cover with the ragù. Sprinkle with freshly grated Pecorino Romano and extra mint for garnish.

Marcello's Favorite
Bucatini con Salsicce

3 tablespoons olive oil
4 links sweet Italian sausage
2 garlic cloves, quartered
2 slices of ¼-inch thick pancetta, diced
2 cans (15 ounces) of chopped tomatoes
1 tablespoon tomato paste
Freshly ground pepper
1 teaspoon kosher salt
Large bunch of fresh parsley, chopped
2 large egg yolks
2 tablespoons heavy cream
1 tablespoon freshly grated Parmeggiano Reggiano,
    plus another ½ cup for serving
1 package bucatini

Heat oil in a medium skillet over medium heat. Remove and discard casings from the sweet Italian sausage and put meat aside.

Add chunks of garlic to medium hot pan. Do not let the garlic burn! When toasted, remove garlic from oil and discard.

Add diced pancetta. Once pancetta has rendered its fat, add sausage. Cook sausage until no longer pink inside.

Add the chopped tomatoes, tomato paste, 1 teaspoon of kosher salt and ground pepper, and ¼ cup of chopped fresh parsley. Simmer for 20 minutes to reduce. You can turn off at this point if needed. Meanwhile, bring a large pot of water to a boil.

In a small bowl, combine egg yolks, heavy cream, and 1 tablespoon of fresh Parmigiano cheese. Set aside.

Once water is boiling, add salt and bucatini. Cook until al dente. This can take longer than other long pastas as it is a bit thicker.

When bucatini is cooked, turn off stove, strain the pasta, and while still piping hot, put back into the pot. Immediately stir in the egg yolk and cream mixture. The heat of the pasta will cook the raw egg as you combine.

Once the egg and cream mixture has been thoroughly combined, add your sausage tomato sauce to the pot. Add a handful of chopped fresh parsley to finish.

For some, soft-shell crabs are an acquired taste. From the crunch of the shell, eating the whole crab, and not being available throughout the entire summer, they're like a limited-edition crab. When I lived in Colorado, seeing them for sale even for two or three weeks in the grocery store in August was like finding a diamond in the rough. I would think, *Wow, soft-shells! Those are a lot smaller than I remember.*

I wanted to share my great find with all of my friends, so I paid a premium for each crab. Most of my Colorado friends didn't know much about soft-shell crabs, so I was faced with explaining how they are the sweet and famous blue crab of the Chesapeake. Unlike other crabs, they are only available for a limited time—when they have molted their exoskeleton and are soft enough to fry and eat whole. Eating them can be a memorable experience, and the pleasure of biting into a forkful of sweet blue crab meat without the hour required to pick out the tiny taste its hard-shelled version allows is unique.

Foods of All Nations in Charlottesville is a wonderful source for soft-shell crabs. While it is recommended to buy them from a fishmonger who keeps them alive, Foods of All Nations sells them cleaned and packaged almost all summer. It might depend on the year, but they are usually large and meaty. It is a great last-minute, easy dinner. No dinner plan? Go to Foods of All Nations. Pick up soft-shell crabs, garlic, and white wine, and you have an elegant, no-prep meal.

If you buy your soft-shell crabs from a fishmonger, I recommend asking to have them cleaned. Soft-shell crabs are often kept alive in the fish case so you receive the freshest product. If you prefer to cut the face off a soft-shell crab yourself, that's always an option. However, if you're like me, you should ask to have them cleaned by the fishmonger—a detail I didn't know the second time I made the following recipe.

The first time I made this recipe, I went to the fishmonger to purchase the crabs. I picked them out of the case, and he wrapped them up and gave them to me. What I did *not* realize was that he cleaned them without being asked. I went home, pan fried my crabs, and had a lovely meal.

The next time, I went back to the same location, but there was a different fishmonger. He took my crab order, wrapped them up, and gave them to me. This set of crabs, however, had been left alive. I opened my packaged crabs and immediately noticed their movement. You might steam hard-shell crabs and live lobsters, but soft-shell crabs are a different story.

By the time I was ready to put the crab in the hot pan, something felt wrong. *How can I be so cruel?* I thought. *A live crab in a hot pan. I don't remember them moving this much before.* Unfortunately, I did it anyway. Telling the crab over and over, "I'm so sorry."

I placed the flour-dusted crab into the hot pan. And it jumped! It hit the ceiling, fell to the floor, and crawled toward the door. I screamed, trying to understand where I went wrong. When I called the fishmonger later, he said that he hadn't cleaned them since I hadn't asked. He was right, and a lesson was learned.

You want your fish to be as fresh as possible until the moment—and this is key—before you cook it. If you know how to clean your soft-shell crab, go for it. Otherwise, if you do not want to go through the process at home, make sure to ask your fishmonger to clean it for you. Or...go to Foods of All Nations, where it's already ready to go.

Soft-Shell Crabs

Pan Fried Soft-Shell Crabs in Garlic Caper Butter

4 soft-shell crabs, cleaned and patted dry
1 cup flour
2 tablespoons extra-virgin olive oil
3 garlic cloves, sliced
2 tablespoons capers, drained
½ cup white wine
1 tablespoon butter
1 scallion, chopped
½ lemon
Salt and freshly ground black pepper

Season crabs with salt and pepper and dredge in the flour, shaking off excess. Set aside.

In a large skillet over medium-high heat, add the oil and pan fry crabs until soft, about 2 minutes on each side. Remove the crabs and set aside. Add the garlic and cook for 1 minute. Then add the capers and white wine. Cook until wine has reduced to about half.

Swirl in butter and chopped scallion. Season with salt and pepper. Squeeze lemon juice as desired.

Fried Green Tomatoes

Fried Green Tomatoes with Warm Crawfish Sauce

While a classic remoulade starts with a mayonnaise base, this recipe is inspired by Emeril Lagasse's take on the classic sauce without the mayo.

The Remoulade

¼ cup freshly squeezed lemon juice
¾ cup vegetable oil
½ cup chopped onions
½ cup chopped scallions (green onions)
¼ cup chopped celery
2 tablespoons prepared horseradish
3 tablespoons Creole or whole-grain mustard
2 tablespoons ketchup
3 tablespoons chopped parsley
Salt
Cayenne pepper

The Crawfish Tails

2 tablespoons butter
½ cup minced onions
½ cup green bell pepper, small dice
1 pound crawfish tails (You can buy frozen and cooked. Defrost the night before.)
Salt and pepper to taste

The Tomatoes

12 slices fresh green tomatoes, about ¼-inch thick
1 cup fine dried bread crumbs
1 cup of cornmeal
1 cup flour
2 large eggs
1 tablespoon milk
Creole seasoning
½ cup vegetable oil for frying
1 tablespoon chopped scallions (green onions) for garnish
Salt and freshly ground black pepper

Creole Seasoning

(yields 1 cup)

You can purchase this already made or make it yourself to adjust seasoning. If you like more heat, add more cayenne. Some like 2–3 tablespoons for a punch.

⅓ cup paprika
3 tablespoons dried oregano
3 tablespoons ground black pepper
2 tablespoons dried basil
2 tablespoons kosher salt
1 tablespoon cayenne pepper
1 tablespoon granulated onion
4 teaspoons dried thyme
4 teaspoons granulated garlic

First, make the remoulade. Combine lemon juice, oil, onions, scallions, celery, horseradish, mustard, ketchup, and parsley in a food processor fitted with a metal blade and process for 30 seconds. Season with salt and cayenne pepper to taste. Use immediately, or store in the refrigerator in an airtight container. Sauce will keep for several days in the refrigerator.

In a large sauté pan over medium heat, melt the butter. Add the onions and bell peppers. Season with salt and pepper. Sauté for 1 minute. Add the crawfish tails and season with salt and pepper. Continue to sauté for 2–3 minutes and then add the remoulade. Bring the mixture to a simmer, and cook for 1 minute. Keep warm over low heat while cooking the tomatoes.

Season the tomatoes with salt and pepper. Set up a breading station. Combine the breadcrumbs and cornmeal in a small bowl. Place the flour in another bowl and the egg wash in a third bowl. Season each bowl with Creole seasoning.

Dredge each slice of tomato in the flour. Then dip each slice in the egg wash, letting the excess drip off. Finally, dredge each slice in the cornmeal/breadcrumb mixture, coating completely.

In a large sauté pan over medium heat, add the oil. When the oil is hot, pan fry the tomatoes in batches until golden and crispy on both sides, about 2–3 minutes. Remove and drain on paper towels. Season with Creole seasoning. Reheat the crawfish sauce.

To serve, lay three tomatoes in the center of each plate. Spoon a quarter of the sauce over each plate of tomatoes. Garnish with scallions.

A beautiful destination along the growing scenic Route 151 in Nelson County, just outside of Charlottesville, is **Bold Rock Hard Cidery.** While this route is a gateway to Virginia's wineries, breweries, and a few distilleries, the flagship, timber-framed Bold Rock Cidery tasting barn in the Rockfish Valley is a must. Saved as an open piece of land for years, it expanded from a small tasting barn to an elegant, rustic, tasting taproom. This spot is an idyllic example of the beauty of this valley, and its owner, John Washburn, has opened it to share with all of us.

The cider barn, which houses the main tasting room and taproom, allows you to see the bottling and brewing process through huge glass windows on one side. The windows in the back reveal the expansive wrap-around deck and scenery that makes you feel like you are in the trees. John has created an elegant yet down to earth, comfortable atmosphere. Dogs are allowed on the deck and patios outside, and everyone can hang out with a cider by the fire pits. The property extends to the Rockfish River, a short walk down the hill, and you are permitted to bring your cider as you stroll the property.

It's a beautiful drive to Bold Rock and a beautiful place to meet, hang out, and try their varieties of hard cider. They include Virginia Apple, Virginia Draft, Apple IPA, Pear Cider, and premium ciders Vat No. 1 and Vintage Dry. They are committed to using Virginia apples and partner with many local orchards. Their cider is a great component of the next recipe.

Bold Rock Clams

Steamed Clams with Chorizo, Fennel, and Bold Rock Hard Cider

2 dozen little neck clams
1 small onion
2 cloves garlic
1 fennel bulb
2 tablespoons olive oil
2 links spicy chorizo (casings removed)
2 bottles or cans of Bold Rock Hard Virginia Apple Cider
1 cup white wine
Pinch of smoked paprika
Chopped fresh parsley

Brush the clams in cold water, remove grit, and rinse in strainer. Chop the onion and slice the garlic. Clean the fennel and remove the core. Slice the fennel bulb, saving fronds for garnish.

Heat olive oil in pan large enough to hold all clams with lid. Add garlic and onion to pan when oil is hot. Be careful not to let them burn. Once both have sweat, add chorizo and cook through. Add fennel, cook until tender or slightly caramelized. Add the Bold Rock Cider and white wine, and stir to loosen any bits from pan. Add clams, and steam with lid on until they open. Once open, add pinch of smoked paprika and handful of fresh parsley and fennel fronds.

Serve immediately with a chunky piece of fresh bread to soak up the cider broth.

Inspired by Aarti Sequeira of the Food Network, this aloo gobi recipe came about when the ingredients of the refrigerator were very low. I had a head of cauliflower and some potatoes to make dinner, and this is exactly the base for the Indian dish aloo gobi. Of course, the spices are what bring out the warm depth of flavor this dish offers with such simple ingredients.

I keep a collection of fresh spices in my cupboard, and it is energizing when you realize you have all the spices you need to create complex flavors. In Charlottesville, the **Spice Diva** on West Main Street is a fantastic resource for stocking your spice collection. Phyllis Hunter, the Spice Diva, helps you find what you need to create your best recipe. I like buying many of my spices whole so I can grind them fresh at home.

Aloo Gobi

2 tablespoons ginger-garlic paste (recipe follows), or 2
    teaspoons grated ginger
1 tablespoon ground coriander
¼ teaspoon turmeric
1 cup water, divided
2 tablespoons peanut oil or ghee
1 large jalapeño pepper, split down the middle, but
  leaving halves attached
1 teaspoon cumin seeds
1 small head cauliflower, cut into small florets
1 russet potato, peeled and cut into ½-inch cubes
(similar size to cauliflower)
kosher salt
½ teaspoon dried fenugreek leaves
2 tablespoons freshly minced cilantro leaves to garnish

First, make the ginger-garlic paste. Combine ½ cup garlic cloves, ½ cup fresh ginger, peeled, and ¼ cup canola oil in a food processor. The fresh ginger should be peeled and cut into ½-inch slices. Blend until it forms a semi-smooth paste.

Mix the ginger-garlic paste, coriander, turmeric, and ½ cup water in a small bowl. This is a simple wet spice mix. Set aside.

In a large pot, warm the oil or ghee over medium-high heat until shimmering but not smoking. Add the jalapeño pepper. Let sweat so the fragrance is released and then add the cumin seeds (Careful: It will sputter).

Add the wet spice mixture. Cook until the paste thickens, deepens in color slightly, and oil oozes out of the perimeter of the sauce, about 2 minutes.

Add the cauliflower and potatoes, stirring to coat the vegetables with the spices. Season with salt and add ½ cup water. Cover and cook over medium heat 8–10 minutes. Then remove the lid, stir, and cook until the cauliflower and potatoes are cooked through to your taste, about 5 minutes. Consider undercooking cauliflower because it will continue to cook while serving.

Add dried fenugreek leaves and let flavor combine 1–2 more minutes. Garnish with cilantro and serve over steamed jasmine rice. You can also buy premade naan to serve with the dish to soak up the flavorful curry.

Quynh Nguyen Col '10

PROGRAM COORDINATOR FOR LORNA SUNDBERG
INTERNATIONAL CENTER

When Quynh Nguyen's parents heard that part of her job at the Lorna Sundberg International Center was to plan cooking programs, they jokingly said it was the main reason she accepted the job offer. She laughs, but there was some truth to it.

Quynh's three main hobbies are food, travel, and learning about different cultures. These hobbies grew into lifelong passions during her undergraduate studies at UVA. She met students from various ethnic backgrounds on Grounds. She also studied abroad in Singapore and India, where she was thrown into new environments. She absorbed everything around her, including food. These experiences taught her how different and similar cultures and their food are to each other. She quickly realized how much more she had to learn about the world.

Quynh feels fortunate to continue her journey of exploring the world at the International Center. The Center's mission is to provide programs and services to enhance the international community experience at UVA and offer opportunities for intercultural enrichment. As program coordinator, Quynh plans social and cultural programs, such as English programs, arts and crafts workshops, movie screenings, dance workshops, and cooking classes to fulfill the center's mission.

Through her work, she constantly meets interesting people from around the world. She considers it a privilege to work with them to showcase aspects of their cultures with the community. With her work, she feels as though she has traveled to many different countries without having to leave Charlottesville.

One of Quynh's favorite parts about working at the Center is the cooking classes. Students, visiting scholars, organizations, community members, and even visiting family members lead the classes. Participants experience new food and learn how to make cultural dishes with unique techniques from a particular country, culture, or family.

For Quynh, another special part about the cooking classes is sharing her Vietnamese heritage and cuisine. When her family moved to the United States in 1996, her parents made it a priority to continue to teach Quynh and her sister about Vietnamese traditions. Quynh carried those traditions with her to UVA and now shares them at the Center.

Braised pork and eggs (thịt kho trứng) is a common comfort food in all regions of Vietnam. It is especially popular during Tết, the Vietnamese Lunar New Year because it is a simple dish to make that lasts for days. Families are very busy during Tết and do not always have time to cook each day, so they often turn to this delicious and convenient dish. Like most Vietnamese braised dishes, this dish is paired with pickled bean sprouts (dưa giá).

Braised Pork and Eggs

Thịt Kho Trứng

(serves 4)

1 pound pork butt/shoulder, cut into 1-inch chunks
1 tablespoon minced garlic
1½ tablespoons minced shallots
½ teaspoon fish sauce (Việt Hương/Three Crabs brand is recommended.)
¼ teaspoon salt
1 teaspoon black pepper
2 tablespoons sugar
1–2 tablespoons water
1½ cups coconut juice (not water, not milk)
6 large eggs

In a medium bowl, mix the pork with garlic, shallots, fish sauce, salt, and pepper. Let it marinate for at least 30 minutes.

To add a golden color to this braised dish, you need to add a caramel sauce (not the same caramel sauce that you drizzle on your ice cream). In a large saucepan on medium heat, add 2 tablespoons of sugar. You'll essentially burn the sugar. Once the sugar is bubbling and has a nice amber color to it, add 1–2 tablespoons of water to liquefy the melted sugar. (Warning: It'll get smoky, so blast your hood fan or open your windows. Otherwise, your smoke detector might go off. I promise—it's worth it!)

Add the marinated pork to the saucepan with the caramelized sugar and brown it evenly. Then add the coconut juice to the pan. Bring to a soft boil and then reduce the heat to low. Cover and cook for 30 minutes.

Hard-boil the eggs while the pork is cooking. Peel the eggs and then poke some holes in them. The holes will help the eggs better absorb the sauce.

After the pork has cooked for 30 minutes, taste the sauce. Add more salt, fish sauce, or pepper to taste. Add the eggs, and cook uncovered for another 30–45 minutes.

Serve with rice and pickled bean sprouts.

Betsy Casteen

The University of Virginia has been a special place for the Casteen family. Betsy Casteen attended Boston Architectural Center and earned a Master's Degree in urban affairs from Boston University. She has been a city planner in Cambridge, Boston, and New York City, where she served in various public and private offices.

In 2003, Betsy married John T. Casteen III, the seventh president of the University of Virginia. She traveled extensively with President Casteen on behalf of UVA to communicate the University's aspirations to alumni, parents, and friends. On many occasions, she represented the president and often spoke on his behalf. In addition to serving as its seventh president for twenty years, John Casteen received three degrees from UVA. Three of their five children, their two sons-in-law, and their daughter-in-law all received degrees from the University of Virginia.

Living at Carr's Hill, the official residence of the president and his family, they enjoyed the everyday hustle and bustle of UVA and many family holidays. Every year around Christmas, the Casteen family still finds their house filled with the blessed cheer of a full house—five grown children, spouses, grandchildren, and dogs. With joy comes the tradition of making cassoulet. John loves this process, and since it may take a couple of days to cook and eat, it involves almost everyone (except the dogs, who are banned to the outdoors).

There are many varieties of cassoulet, but all are based on the French casserole, which includes numerous ingredients, such as duck, pork, sausage, and white beans. After a lot of trial and error with various recipes, the Casteens have found this recipe, adapted from *Saveur*, to be the most satisfying. It is said that the dish is from southwestern France, and since John has ancestors from the Pau region, it makes sense that his taste buds call for this as a celebratory meal. With a houseful of chefs, sous chefs, and eaters, the time involved is well worth it.

Casteen Cassoulet

Adapted from Saveur

(serves 8–10)

1 pound dried white beans, soaked overnight and drained
4 ounces slab bacon, cut into 4 pieces
2 teaspoons whole black peppercorns
1 teaspoon whole cloves
8 sprigs thyme
6 sprigs parsley
2 bay leaves
Cheesecloth for herbs (bouquet garni)
2 boneless, skin-on duck breasts
½ pound duck sausage
2 duck legs, drumsticks and thighs separated
Kosher salt and freshly ground black pepper to taste
10 cloves garlic, peeled and smashed
2 large yellow onions, thinly sliced
2 cups duck or chicken stock
2 legs duck confit, homemade or store bought, skin and bones
    discarded, and meat shredded
1 can (28 ounces) whole peeled tomatoes in purée,
    crushed by hand
3 tablespoons duck fat
1 cup fresh bread crumbs

Pour the beans into a large pot. Add the bacon and enough water to cover the beans by about 2 inches. Tie the peppercorns, cloves, thyme, parsley, and bay leaves in the cheesecloth and add. Bring to a boil on medium-high heat. Reduce to medium-low and cook, covered slightly, until beans are tender, about 90 minutes. Discard the bouquet garni, and transfer the beans and cooking liquid to a bowl. Cover with plastic wrap, and set aside.

Season the duck breasts with salt. Wipe the pan dry. Place the breasts skin side down, and heat over medium-high heat. Cook without flipping until fat is rendered and skin is crisp, 5–6 min-

utes. Transfer to a cutting board and set aside.

Cook sausage, flipping once, until browned, about 3–4 minutes. Transfer to a cutting board and slice ½-inch thick on an angle; set aside.

Season drumsticks and thighs with salt and pepper. Working in batches, cook, turning as needed, until fat is rendered, and duck is browned, about 5–7 minutes.

Transfer to a plate and set aside. Add garlic and onions to pan. Cook, stirring occasionally, until golden, about 15 minutes.

Return sausage, drumsticks, and thighs to pan and add stock, confit, tomatoes, salt, and pepper. Bring to a boil and then reduce heat to medium. Cook until duck is tender, about 60–90 minutes. Using a slotted spoon, transfer sausage, drumsticks, thighs, and confit to a bowl; reserve broth.

Assemble the cassoulet. Preheat oven to 375°F. Rub an 8-quart Dutch oven with 2 tablespoons duck fat. Using a slotted spoon, transfer ⅓ of the beans to the pot. Add half the sausage, drumsticks, thighs, and confit. Add another ⅓ of the beans and then the remaining sausage, drumsticks, thighs, and confit. Top with the remaining beans, and pour 1 cup of the reserved broth over the top.

Slice duck breasts ¼-inch thick on an angle, and arrange over the top. Melt remaining duck fat in a 1-quart saucepan. Stir in the bread crumbs, salt, and pepper.

Sprinkle the bread crumb mixture over top of the dish, and place in the oven. Bake until cassoulet is bubbling, about 40 minutes. Increase heat to 450°F. Cook until bread crumbs are browned, about 3–5 minutes. Take out of oven and let sit 10 minutes.

Dabney Gough Col '99

Although Dabney grew up just sixty miles away in Lynchburg, Virginia, Charlottesville felt like a world away. It offered so many new eating experiences: Café Europa, with its creamy tomato soup and crusty baguettes, the cheese plate at the C&O, and the fascinating aisles at Foods of All Nations. Not to mention the endless variety of foods cooked by fellow residents at Mosaic House, the multicultural community at Hoxton House, where Dabney lived in her third and fourth years as an undergrad.

She pursued her degree in anthropology, and after graduating (class of '99), headed to the West Coast to start her adult life in San Francisco. Like many recent grads in late '90s San Francisco, Dabney found herself working at a series of dot.com companies. Eventually, the appeal of foosball and margarita Fridays faded, and she pined for a more meaningful career that fed her passions. So, she quit her job doing website usability research and enrolled in culinary school.

At the same time, she found an after-school job at Bi-Rite Market, a specialty grocery and deli with the bonus of being on the same block where Dabney lived. It was there that Dabney started to learn about local and organic fruits and vegetables, humanely raised meats, and sustainably harvested fish and seafood.

After a few years, Dabney yearned for a change of scenery and moved back to the East Coast, where she found a job in the test kitchen at *Fine Cooking* magazine. There she learned the rigorous practice of writing and testing recipes, skills that turned out to be very useful in later writing projects. About a year later, she moved back to San Francisco to rejoin the Bi-Rite team once again.

It was through Bi-Rite that she had the opportunity to co-author two cookbooks based on Bi-Rite businesses. The first, *Eat Good Food: A Grocer's Guide to Shopping, Cooking, and Creating Community through Food* (Ten Speed Press, 2011), is a grocery shopping guide with recipes. The second was an ice cream how-to—*Sweet Cream & Sugar Cones: 90 Recipes for Making Your Own Ice Cream and Frozen Treats* (Ten Speed Press, 2012).

Now, she celebrates and promotes good food at Whole Foods Market with her husband, fellow UVA alum and writer Tyler McMahon, in Hawaii. In her marketing role, she celebrates the amazing variety of locally grown fruits, vegetables, meats, and seafood and helps consumers understand the impact of making good food choices.

Most recently, Dabney started a project to explore her interest in other people's food careers. Her podcast, *Tasty Grinds*, offers monthly (or so) interviews with people who have unusual or interesting food-related jobs. Guests have included a restaurant critic, a shipboard cook, and fellow UVA alum Todd Pontius, who fuels his own passion as an artisanal cheesemaker.

According to Dabney, her pork recipe is an homage to some of Virginia's best fall foods—from apples to collard greens, even grapes by way of white wine! The slow-braised pork takes a bit of time, but it's nearly all hands-off and has delicious results. You'll end up with way more pork than you will need to serve with the veggies, but if you're going to go to the trouble of braising, you might as well make the most of it with a big cut. You'll have plenty of leftovers for sandwiches, tacos, and more. For best results, seek pork from small, sustainably focused operations, such as the amazing EcoFriendly Foods in Moneta, Virginia.

Wine-Braised Pork
Wine-Braised Pork with Sautéed Apples, Fennel, and Collard Greens

6 pounds boneless pork butt (also known as shoulder)

2 tablespoons fat of choice, such as rendered lard, olive oil, vegetable oil, or even coconut oil (Do not use butter unless it is clarified.)

Kosher salt

10 peppercorns

6 large garlic cloves, smashed and peeled

1 bay leaf

½ bottle dry white wine (Virginia wine is best, of course!)

1 medium fennel bulb, cored and sliced into ¼-inch thick wedges, about 2 cups (Freeze any stalks and fronds for stock, but if you have fronds, save a few for garnish.)

½ large yellow onion, peeled and sliced into ¼-inch thick wedges, about 1½ cups

1 tart baking apple (Granny Smith is good), cored and cut into ¼-inch wedges, about 1½ cups

1 bunch of tender collard greens (about 11 leaves, no more than 10 inches across), stemmed, halved lengthwise, and cut into ⅓-inch ribbons, about 3½ packed cups

3 tablespoons fat of choice, such as rendered lard, olive oil, vegetable oil, or even coconut oil (Do not use butter unless it is clarified.)

½ teaspoon ground mustard seed

1 tablespoon apple cider vinegar, Sherry vinegar, or fresh lemon juice

Prepare the pork. If the pork has a layer of fat or skin, use a sharp knife to score a crosshatch pattern in 1½-inch intervals. Use butcher twine to tie the roast in 2–3 places to keep the roast compact so it will cook uniformly.

Pat the pork dry and sprinkle with 2 tablespoons salt. Let it sit at room temperature for about 1 hour to season and come to room temperature.

When you are ready to cook the pork, preheat the oven to 250°F. Heat a large Dutch oven over medium-high heat. Add the fat and swirl to coat the bottom of the pan. Add the pork, skin side down if there's skin. Let sear undisturbed for at least 3 minutes. Then use tongs to gently lift the pork. If it sticks to the pan, let it sear in place for another couple of minutes before trying again. Turn and repeat on all sides until it is golden all over. If it seems to darken very quickly, or if the bottom of the pan starts to accumulate charred spots, reduce the heat. Lastly, turn the pork so it's standing on a short end; you want to make some room in the bottom of the pan.

Add the peppercorns, garlic, and bay leaf to the pan. Sauté for 1–2 minutes just to release the flavors. Put the pork skin side up, add the wine, and bring to a boil. Cover the pot, turn off the heat, and transfer the pot to the oven.

Check the pot after 20 minutes. If the liquid is boiling rapidly, reduce the heat. Cook for 2–3 hours, or until the pork is very tender. (Test it by inserting a fork and pulling gently; the meat should separate with little force.) Remove from the oven, and set aside to cool in the liquid.

While the pork is braising, prep the vegetables for the sauté.

Heat a large skillet over medium-high heat. Add 2 tablespoons of the fat, and swirl to coat. Add fennel, onions, and ½ teaspoon salt. Cook, stirring frequently, until they start to become translucent and brown on the edges.

Add the apples, mustard seed, and ¼ cup of the braising liquid. Sauté just until the apples start to soften, 2–3 minutes. Don't overcook; you want them to maintain some bite. Transfer mixture to a bowl.

You can make this apple-onion mixture ahead of time and pick up here just before serving.

Lower the heat to medium. Heat another tablespoon of in the pan, and add the collards. Toss constantly for 1–2 minutes, or until they start to brighten in color. Add ¼ cup of the braising liquid. Toss and stir just until greens start to wilt. Add the apples and onions. Gently toss to mix, and heat everything through.

Turn off the heat, add the vinegar or lemon juice, and mix. Taste and season with additional salt if necessary.

Remove the pork from the liquid and either slice into ½-inch slabs or pull apart into chunks with a fork. Serve over the greens and drizzle a little more braising liquid over the top. Garnish with fennel fronds if you have them.

Put any pork you aren't eating back in the braising liquid to cool and store; it will stay juicier that way. Once the pork is gone, don't throw away the braising liquid. Strain and save it for a delicious soup base. It freezes beautifully, too.

You can make the sautéed veggies as a standalone dish. Use an equal amount of water or stock in place of the braising liquid.

James & Kelly King Col '07, NURS '08
CO-OWNERS OF KING FAMILY VINEYARDS

James King, who is originally from Houston, Texas, graduated from the University of Virginia in 2007 with a degree in history and played lacrosse for the Cavaliers. He separated from the U.S. Marine Corps after serving two combat tours overseas. He enjoys hunting and fishing and is currently helping his brothers manage the farm and vineyard after serving as the tasting room manager for a year and general manager for two years at King Family Vineyards.

Kelly King, originally from Mound, Minnesota, also graduated from the University of Virginia with a degree in nursing in 2008. Kelly separated from the U.S. Navy after caring for wounded warriors and serving in the neonatal intensive care unit (NICU) at the San Diego Naval Hospital. After working briefly at the University of Virginia in the NICU, Kelly has recently moved into the role of full-time mom and part-time nurse at Martha Jefferson Hospital. She enjoys taking care of babies, baking bread, crocheting, and taking walks with her dogs, Gunner and Charger. Kelly and James are the proud parents of David "Connor" and Charlotte Lucille King.

While in the service, James and Kelly were stationed in Southern California, just outside San Diego, where they fell in love with the beautiful weather, delicious food, and laid-back culture. An ideal day for them consisted of eating fish tacos, drinking local craft beer, and hanging out with friends on the beach.

Once they left military service and moved back to Virginia, their love of sharing good food and drink with friends never left them. Working in the wine industry has definitely refined their palates and helped them learn more about pairing foods with drinks. James and Kelly feel blessed to live in Albemarle County, Virginia. Not only is it a beautiful place with a vibrant and growing craft beverage industry, but the food scene is also phenomenal.

Asian Salmon

Asian Salmon in Foil

¼ cup honey
3 cloves garlic, minced
2 tablespoons reduced-sodium soy sauce
1 tablespoon seasoned rice vinegar
1 tablespoon sesame oil
1 tablespoon freshly grated ginger
1 teaspoon Sriracha, optional
Freshly ground black pepper to taste
2 pounds salmon
2 scallions (green onions), thinly sliced
½ teaspoon sesame seeds

Preheat oven to 375°F. Line a baking sheet with foil.

In a small bowl, whisk together honey, garlic, soy sauce, rice vinegar, sesame oil, ginger, Sriracha (if using), and pepper to taste.

Place salmon on the prepared baking sheet, and fold up all 4 sides of the foil. Spoon the honey mixture over the salmon. Fold the sides of the foil over the salmon, covering completely and sealing the packet closed.

Place into oven and bake until cooked through, about 15–20 minutes. Open the packet and broil for 2–3 minutes, or until caramelized and slightly charred.

Serve immediately, garnished with scallions and sesame seeds, if desired.

Optional Wine Pairing

King Family Vineyards Crosé. The dry, Merlot-based rosé is fresh and crisp with notes of grapefruit, lime, watermelon, and a light grassiness on the nose. Throughout the palate, a lifting acidity carries flavors of bitter cherry, peach, and rose petal. Very friendly with lighter fare, this wine is also a great companion for the porch or patio.

Andy McClure Com '01

OWNER OF THE VIRGINIAN RESTAURANT

Andy McClure grew up in Alexandria, Virginia, and graduated from UVA with a finance degree from the McIntire School of Commerce ('01). While in school, Andy waited tables at local restaurants. He was an okay server, but he was an even better debater. After months of hearing how he would do things differently and jokes about buying the restaurant, the owners of the tiny but venerable Virginian started to take him seriously. In August 2001, at the ripe old age of 22, Andy became a restaurant owner.

A consummate optimist and burgeoning pragmatist, he spent the first year of ownership thinking he could work his finance job in New York and be an absentee owner of the Virginian. For any restaurateurs out there, they know how ridiculous that sounds. It didn't take long for him to come back. And when he did, restaurants became his life.

It took a long time for the Virginian to find its groove, but its eventual success allowed him to open a second restaurant. Once that addition became stable, Andy began work on purchasing and renovating the Biltmore, another restaurant he worked at in college, to build the largest outdoor bar and patio area in town.

All of this led to Citizen Burger Bar, a restaurant concept Andy always wanted to try and a place whose success and reception has been profoundly humbling. According to Andy, his newest concepts—Tavern & Grocery and Lost Saint— continue to build stylish and fun experiences within historic settings.

Andy's company is employee focused. He believes the best restaurant and business owners realize that their employees are more important than they are. Finding and guiding good people make this company what it is. Andy can't thank all of his employees and all of his guests enough.

The Virginian is *famous* for its Stumble Down Mac 'n Cheese—named after the pool hall that used to reside underneath the restaurant. To make this delicious dish, the Virginian exclusively uses cavatappi pasta, which is bigger and sturdier than macaroni. They cook the pasta al dente and then add it to a saucepan with cream, pepper jack cheese, and salt and pepper to taste. The mac 'n cheese is put in a crock bowl and topped with a cheddar potato cake. Each dish is made to order, and they recommend mixing the crunchy potato cake into the mac. It's the perfect cure for whatever ails you.

Stumble Down
Mac 'n Cheese

2 ounces cavatappi pasta
4 ounces heavy cream
2 ounces Pepper Jack cheese
Salt and pepper to taste

Cheddar Potato Cake
Large handful of shredded potatoes
1 slice cheddar cheese
1 tablespoon diced yellow onion
1 tablespoon diced green pepper
½ ounce flour
½ a large egg
Dash of kosher salt and black pepper

Cook pasta in boiling water until al dente, about 5–7 minutes. Drain and set aside.

In a medium saucepan over medium-high heat, combine heavy cream, Pepper Jack cheese, and salt and pepper to taste. Reduce the cream, and mix in the pasta.

To make a potato cake, preheat a convection oven to 325°F.

Combine all ingredients in a mixing bowl. Fashion into a circle and bake for 10 minutes.

Cool, wrap, and refrigerate. Fry for 1–2 minutes or until brown before topping the mac 'n cheese.

Place mac 'n cheese in a soup bowl, top with potato cake, and serve.

L. F. Payne Darden '73

Lewis Franklin (L. F.) Payne graduated from UVA's Darden School of Business with an MBA. And he's not the only one in his family. In fact, two of his children, Graham and Hunter, are UVA undergrads, and three of his children are Darden MBA graduates, Graham, Hunter, and Anna. His daughter-in-law, Jennifer, has an undergraduate and master's degree from UVA, and his son-in-law, Alex, has an MBA from Darden as well. That's four children and spouses and eight degrees from UVA.

L. F. Payne has been a guest lecturer in the political science department and Darden over the years and has served on the board of the Darden Foundation. In addition, he was a member of the Board of Visitors for eight years and served as the chairman of the Buildings and Grounds Committee. He is also a former member of the United States House of Representatives from the Commonwealth of Virginia. He served the 5th district of the state from June 14, 1988 to January 3, 1997. L. F. is currently the chairman of the UVA Foundation and a board member of the UVA Medical Center.

L. F. and his wife, Susan, live in a restored home that was originally the national headquarters of Kappa Sigma, which many UVA students have no doubt visited. He is president of McGuire-Woods Consulting, with offices in Washington, Richmond, Chicago, Austin, Atlanta, Brussels, and Bucharest, so he and Susan travel frequently. They enjoy the good cuisine and eating experiences discovered in their travels, as well as at home in Charlottesville.

Susan's expertise is in marketing and advertising. She founded her agency The Blue Ridge Group in 2017 after having previously run Payne, Ross & Associates. She also serves as the chairwoman of the Virginia Board of Tourism, working with Virginia's restaurants, wineries, craft beer makers, and more.

When they have some time in Charlottesville, they enjoy cooking on their grill and eating outside. Hence, the following recipe...

Grilled Honey Mustard Chicken

(serves 4)

½ cup any whole-grain mustard
½ cup honey
Juice of ½ lemon
1 garlic clove, smashed and minced
½ teaspoon paprika
½ teaspoon kosher salt
¼ teaspoon cayenne pepper
¼ teaspoon red pepper flakes
4 boneless, skinless chicken breasts

Whisk all ingredients except the chicken breasts in a small bowl.

Reserve 6 tablespoons of sauce, and pour the rest over the chicken. Toss, cover with plastic wrap, and let sit for about 30 minutes at room temperature.

Preheat the grill on medium to medium-high heat. Grill chicken for 6–7 minutes per side, or until done.

Pour the reserved 6 tablespoons of sauce over chicken. Cover loosely with foil, and let rest for about 5 minutes.

Keisha John

DIRECTOR OF DIVERSITY PROGRAMS,
OFFICE OF GRADUATE AND POSTDOCTORAL AFFAIRS

Keisha John joined the academic staff at UVA in January 2015 as Director of Diversity Programs in the Office of Graduate and Postdoctoral Affairs. In this role, she collaborates with partners across Grounds to recruit and support matriculated students who are traditionally underrepresented in their fields.

Many people are surprised to learn, especially when they eat out or she makes desserts, that she is a vegan. Although there are no vegan restaurants in Charlottesville, most have at least one vegan item on their menus. She is very creative with the food she makes, always experimenting with various recipes. It must be the recovering scientist in her.

Keisha is from the school of simple vegan cooking, using what one would find in a typical pantry and replacing or leaving out the eggs, meat, and dairy. She relishes living in Charlottesville, given the abundance of fresh local produce. She recently joined the Little Hat Creek Farm CSA and now receives a weekly basket of local organic vegetables and a loaf of vegan bread, which she promptly splits with friends as the share feeds a family.

Some of Keisha's staple dishes include pesto pasta with regular pasta, squash/zucchini mixture, or parsnips/sweet potato mixture; guacamole and salsa; chana masala or chickpea curry with cous-cous; German mushrooms and polenta with a dab of pesto; simple kale salad; and vegan chocolate chip or kitchen sink cookies.

Vegan Pesto
Vegan Pesto Pasta for All

2 cups or 2 large bunches of fresh basil leaves (can substitute ¼
    with spinach or kale)
½ cup pine nuts or walnuts
¾ cup olive oil
1 head of garlic
½ cup nutritional yeast
1 teaspoon salt
1 teaspoon black pepper

Lightly toast the pine nuts and garlic.

Place all ingredients in a food processor. Pulse for 3–5 minutes, or until everything is mixed and finely chopped. Taste and add additional salt and pepper as needed. You can also add additional oil if you prefer a sauce to paste.

This can be saved for months. Place in an ice tray, freeze overnight, remove the frozen cubes, and store in a freezer bag in the freezer. Use for pasta (see below), as a base on pizza instead of tomato sauce, on scrambled eggs, or on tofu; the uses are limitless.

Use the pesto sauce/paste on penne pasta, spiraled raw zucchini, squash, or a mixture of raw sweet potato and parsnips. Regardless of which you choose, use a generous amount of pesto to coat the pasta. If you made the paste, add additional oil as you coat the pasta.

The zucchini/squash mixture has the least number of calories. However, it takes at least 1 hour for the veggies to absorb the sauce. The raw sweet potato/parsnip mixture has a bit of a crunch, but it is great.

Eric Skokan Col '93

Chef Eric Skokan is one of the most ambitious farm-to-table restaurateurs in America. In fact, he grows most of the food for his two restaurants on 130 acres in Boulder County, Colorado.

Eric, a Virginia native, graduated from UVA in 1993 with a degree in history. He got the cooking bug while working in Charlottesville kitchens as an undergraduate. After graduating, Eric worked in restaurants in Washington, D.C., San Francisco, and Colorado before moving to Boulder and opening his first restaurant, Black Cat Bistro, in 2006.

Shortly after opening Black Cat, an exquisite fine-dining destination, Eric began experimenting with gardening. Small-scale, backyard gardening soon became a passion, and he expanded from a plot in the yard to an acre of vegetables to the current operation, which grows 250 varieties of vegetables, grains, and legumes and raises sheep, heritage pigs, chickens, geese, and more. The livestock operation involves a Turkish breed of guard dog called an Akbash and a llama named Belle. Together, they protect the herd of chickens and more than 100 sheep.

In 2012, Eric opened Bramble & Hare, located next door to Black Cat Bistro. Bramble & Hare is a convivial restaurant with a lively bar and a charming farmhouse decor. Like Black Cat Bistro, the restaurant draws inspiration from the fields. The menus at both restaurants change every night, truly reflecting seasonality like few other restaurants in America.

Eric works closely with Auguste Escoffier School of Culinary Arts in Boulder, which every year sends students to learn about farm-to-table techniques on Black Cat Farm. In 2014, Kyle Books published Eric's book *Farm, Fork, Food: A Year of Spectacular Recipes Inspired by Black Cat Farm*.

 This year, Chef Eric's farm-to-table operation will be the first that is certified as both organic and biodynamic.

From the beginning, Black Cat Farm has been an exercise in experimentation. Eric attributes some of his approach to farming and cooking to the Jeffersonian ideals he absorbed while in Charlottesville. Jefferson championed the self-sufficient yeoman farmer as an exemplary American archetype, and Eric—who learned his way around professional kitchens and in fields by doing and experimenting—keeps the great Thomas Jefferson in mind as he builds his own flour mill, tries to grow artichokes in Colorado (a challenge!), writes a cookbook, and learns how to use dogs and a llama to protect livestock.

Eric lives in a farmhouse on three acres in Boulder County with his wife, Jill, four children, and a whole lot of animals.

Grilled Lamb

Grilled Lamb with Fattoush and Cucumber Yogurt

(serves 4)

3 fresh pita breads
1 tablespoon olive oil
Sea salt
2½ cups of sliced heirloom tomatoes
½ fennel bulb, shaved thin
1 cup of crumbled feta cheese
1 small red onion, cut into small pieces
1 cup of chopped fresh cilantro

½ cup fresh mint, minced
½ cup chopped fresh basil
½ cup diced pitted Kalamata olives
1 cucumber, seeded and grated
2 cups plain yogurt
3 tablespoons minced fresh parsley
Freshly ground black pepper
2 tablespoons extra-virgin olive oil
2 pounds lamb sirloin, trimmed

Photo taken by Melissa when she was given a tour of Chef Eric's farm just outside of Boulder, Colorado.

Brush the pita breads with olive oil and season with salt. Grill over charcoal or wood fire until lightly charred, about 1 minute each side, or toast under broiler. Tear into bite-sized pieces, and transfer to a large bowl. Toss the pieces of pita with the tomatoes, fennel, feta, onion, cilantro, ½ cup of the mint, basil, and olives. Season with salt to taste.

In a small bowl, toss together cucumber, yogurt, remainder of mint, and parsley. Season with salt and pepper, and stir in the extra-virgin olive oil.

Season the lamb with salt. Grill over charcoal or wood fire until lightly charred and cooked to desired doneness, about 5 minutes each side. Season with pepper. Transfer lamb to a platter to rest for 10 minutes and then slice thinly.

Divide the lamb among four plates. Top each with fattoush and cucumber yogurt. Serve immediately.

Recipe adapted from *Farm, Fork, Food: A Year of Spectacular Recipes Inspired by Black Cat Farm*.

Harrison Keevil Col '05

KEEVIL & KEEVIL GROCERY

When Harrison Keevil was at UVA, he studied foreign affairs with a focus on Western Europe. Being half-British, Harrison felt a natural desire to study this topic because it might be a way to work in London. After graduating, Harrison did just that by becoming a research assistant to The Right Honorable John Whittingdale.

However, when in London, a funny thing happened. Harrison fell in love with food and, more importantly, cooking. After his first fine-dining experience, Harrison knew he wanted to become a chef.

Fast-forward five years with stops in New York City, San Francisco, and London again, Harrison found himself working at the Clifton Inn in Charlottesville under then-chef Dean Maupin. It was there that Harrison began to learn all the local farms and artisan makers. Because of his time in London and San Francisco, and having grown up working on an organic cattle farm in Goochland, Virginia, Harrison wanted to cook with as many local ingredients as possible.

While at Clifton, Harrison met his future wife, Jennifer. Before they were even married, and with a lot of naïveté, they opened Brookville Restaurant in July of 2010. Focusing on local sourcing, Harrison and Jennifer worked with many area farms to bring in ingredients for both the food and drink menus. Some of the farms they worked with include Timbercreek Farm, Sharondale Farm, Caromont Farm, and Local Food Hub. In addition, Brookville's bar featured only beer, wine, and spirits from Virginia. If it grows together, it goes together.

It is Harrison and Jennifer's hope that local food will become more the norm and not just seen as a luxury good. They want to work to allow anyone interested to try the spoils of central Virginia.

Now running Keevil & Keevil Grocery and Kitchen in the Belmont neighborhood in Charlottesville, Harrison and Jennifer are committed to creating a low-carbon footprint in our community. They compost and recycle every day, use local farms and gardens, and create pickles, salsas, and jellies with their leftover produce.

When at home, Harrison and Jennifer cook most of their meals. With two little girls to feed, there are the staple mac and cheese and chicken tender nights. However, a lot of the time, either Jennifer is cooking up one of her go-to dishes or Harrison is sparking up the grill. Harrison and Jennifer love to shop at the locally owned grocery options in town because they all have great local options. They include Timbercreek Market, Foods of All Nations, Feast!, and Reids.

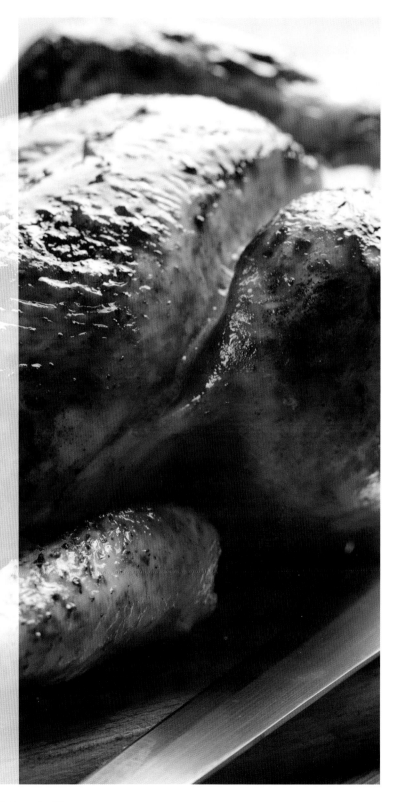

Roasted Chicken

1 whole chicken (3–4 pounds)
2 sprigs thyme
2 sprigs rosemary
½ lcmon
1 clove garlic, cut in half
Salt and pepper to taste

Preheat the oven to 375°F. Wash and dry the chicken.
Liberally season the cavity of the chicken with salt and
pepper. Stuff the thyme, rosemary, lemon, and garlic into
the cavity. Truss the chicken. Season the skin of the chicken
with salt and pepper.

Place the chicken in the oven for 1 hour. Insert a meat
thermometer into the thigh. If it does not read 165°F, place
the chicken back in the oven. Check every 10 minutes until
it is ready. When the thermometer reads 165°F, pull the
chicken out of the oven, and allow it to rest for at least 20
minutes before carving it.

Serve the chicken family-style with your favorite side
dishes. Any leftover meat is great for chicken sandwiches.

Kim Kirschnick

CAVMAN

Most people call him "Cavman," but his name is Kim Kirschnick. His career as Cavman began in 1994, when the UVA Promotions Department was looking to boost enthusiasm through the mounted Cavalier. It started as a photo shoot in a field off Garth Road. It ended up being the football poster for the 1994 season.

Fast-forward to 2000. Kim was asked if he had a horse that could handle the crowds, noise, and excitement of UVA football to resurrect the mounted Cavalier. Kim plays polo as a hobby, and at the time, he had 10 or 12 horses. So, he loaded them up and auditioned each one to see which had the best mind, look, and ability to handle the task. "I still have one of my retired football horses, Trinda, who turned 28 in April."

Kim considers it an honor to be a part of UVA athletics. He particularly enjoys the excitement of young children and the dedication of the longtime fans. "Being Cavman is the best job in the world. Where else, as a grown man, do you get to wear a cape and ride a horse with a real sword?"

Kim lives in Ivy with his wife, Debra, four horses—Sabre, Hoppy, Atoka, and Trinda—and hunting dog, Bandit, who also enjoys attending the games!

Cavman Lasagna

1 medium white onion, chopped
4–5 fresh garlic cloves, diced
1 medium green bell pepper, chopped
4 tablespoons olive oil
4 teaspoons dried Italian seasonings
4 tablespoons fresh Italian parsley
1½ pounds high-quality ground beef
1½ pounds bulk Italian sausage
1 teaspoon kosher salt
½ teaspoon pepper
1 teaspoon garlic powder
1 can (28 ounces) diced tomatoes with juice
1 can (6 ounces) tomato paste
1 can (15 ounce) tomato sauce
Uncooked lasagna noodles
3 cups shredded mozzarella cheese
3 cups shredded Parmesan cheese
2 cups ricotta cheese

Place first 4 ingredients into large Dutch oven on medium heat. Sauté until translucent. Add Italian seasoning, parsley, ground beef, and Italian sausage. Brown thoroughly.

Add salt, pepper, and garlic powder. Add tomatoes with juice, tomato paste, and tomato sauce. Reduce the heat to simmer, and cook for about 45 minutes, checking to make sure that mixture does not dry out. Add a small amount of water if necessary. Remove from heat.

Preheat oven to 350°F. In a 9×13 baking dish, layer the following in the baking dish. Line the bottom with ⅓ of the lasagna noodles. Layer ⅓ of the meat/sauce mixture on top of noodles. Spread ⅓ of the ricotta cheese in dollops across meat/sauce mixture layer. Follow with a layer of ⅓ of the mozzarella cheese and a layer of ⅓ of the Parmesan cheese. Repeat twice. Make sure you end with a meat/sauce layer and then top with all the cheeses.

Cover with aluminum foil and bake for 1 hour. Remove foil and brown the top layer on broil for about 2 minutes. Allow lasagna to set for about 5 minutes before cutting into casserole.

Can be frozen.

The Catering Outfit
Walter Slawski Col '99

Walter Theo Xavier Slawski first encountered UVA while commuting to boarding school at Woodberry Forest from Harare, Zimbabwe. He accepted early admission to the University and began his undergraduate study in economics. Walter worked in local restaurants and catering companies, learning everything from front of house to culinary artistry.

Having entered UVA with twenty-six credits, Walter found himself with a light course load in his fourth year. So, he decided to fly the coop and start his own catering service. In January of 1999, he received his health department certification and opened the doors.

By the fall of the following year, **The Catering Outfit** was providing daily meals for nineteen of the twenty-six Greek organizations affiliated with UVA at the time. It was awarded the contract to provide both preseason and in-season meals to the University's football team under George Welsh.

The Catering Outfit has evolved over the years, finally settling in 2003 at the home of Walter's first restaurant, the Shebeen Pub and Braai. Walter calls the Shebeen a culinary interpretation of his African childhood. During the restaurant's thirteen-year (and counting!) tenure in the competitive Charlottesville restaurant scene, Shebeen has become a locally born Charlottesville icon.

Charlottesville has become one of the leading wedding destination locations on the East Coast, and Walter decided to reshape The Catering Outfit into its go-to caterer for discerning clients. His work has been published in leading industry magazines and blogs, including *Weddings Unveiled, Southern Weddings*, the *Ruffled* blog, *Carats and Cake, Cville Weddings, Borrowed and Blue,* and *Charlottesville Wine and Country Weddings*.

Both The Catering Outfit and the Shebeen are very active in the local community, contributing to fundraising efforts, including Silver Linings blood drive, the University cancer center, Makindu Children's Program, Pure Madi, Martha's Market, Ronald McDonald House, Women in Sports, UVA Cancer Center, and the V Foundation. Walter is proud and grateful to be a UVA alumnus who has the great fortune to live and work in his alma mater's town!

Confit Pork Belly

Confit Pork Belly with Pomegranate Gastrique and Kalette Salad

Note: This is a professional recipe and for the ambitious home cook only. The Chinese five spice cured pork will take a total of 40 hours.

(serves 12)

Roast Pork
½ cup fresh garlic, minced
18 bay leaves, crushed
2 tablespoons fresh thyme, stemmed and chopped
6 tablespoons sea salt

2 tablespoons coriander, toasted and ground
1 tablespoon coarsely ground black pepper
1½ teaspoons Chinese five spice
8 pounds bone-in local pork shoulder
5 pounds lard (manteca, or rendered pork fat; you can use this again and again)

First, make the dry brine. In the bowl of a food processor, combine garlic, bay leaves, thyme, salt, coriander, pepper, and Chinese five spice. Pulse until uniformly incorporated.

Using a sharp boning knife, remove bone from shoulder. Butterfly boneless shoulder to achieve a flat, uniform product. Rub dry brine evenly over all surfaces of shoulder. Place on baking sheet, and cover with plastic wrap, pressing film firmly against shoulder. There should be as little air as possible. Refrigerate for 24 hours.

When ready to cook, preheat oven to 200°F. Heat lard in a deep, 8-quart roasting pan until translucent. Remove shoulder from refrigerator. Unwrap, and submerge in lard. Place in oven for 12 hours.

Carefully remove roast from the oven and the lard. Strain the lard, and refrigerate for future deliciousness. Wrap pork in plastic, and place between two pans to press. Place a heavy item on top to weigh down the pork. Ratchet straps can be used to press the pans together.

Place weighted pork in refrigerator until cold (at least 4 hours). Once chilled, cut pork into 4-ounce portions (roughly 2-inch squares). Heat grill or griddle on high. Sear both sides of the pork portions. Remove to baking sheet and reserve.

CONTINUED ON PAGE 80...

Pomegranate Gastrique

4 whole pomegranates, juiced, or 2 cups pomegranate juice
1 cup apple cider vinegar
½ cup light brown sugar

If using whole pomegranates, pass juice through fine-mesh sieve. Combine ingredients in a saucepan over medium heat. Reduce volume by half. Remove from heat, and cool on counter to room temperature. Gastrique should be thick and syrupy.

Grits

4 quarts water
¼ cup grapeseed oil or other high-quality vegetable oil
2 tablespoons kosher salt
1 quart local stoneground grits
½ cup heavy cream
1 pound local Taleggio-style cheese, shredded
1 pound local Gouda-style cheese, shredded
1 pound local Manchego-style cheese, shredded

Combine water, oil, and salt in a shallow, 6-quart saucepan on high heat. Add grits and stir. Heat to boiling, about 15 minutes, stirring regularly. Reduce heat to low, and simmer, stirring regularly, until grits are tender and slightly firm in consistency, about 1 hour. (*Chef's Note:* When stirring [I used a wooden spoon], keep in contact with the bottom of the pot to prevent sticking. You may have to scrape the bottom.) Add heavy cream and cheese, stirring to incorporate. Remove from heat and keep warm.

Kalette Salad with Dressing

1 pound local hickory-slab bacon
4 packages (1½ pound) Kalettes
1 pound purple pear onions, peeled
1 pound French beans, snipped
1 whole pomegranate, seeded for arils
4 clementines, peeled and sectioned
1 cup grapeseed oil
1 cup local apple cider
¾ cup apple cider vinegar
¼ cup Dijon mustard
1 tablespoon local honey
1 tablespoon sea salt
1 teaspoon black pepper
½ cup rendered bacon fat
½ cup shallots, diced

Preheat the oven to 350° F. Cut bacon into ¼-inch thick slices. Place on a rack in a flat rimmed baking sheet. Cook for 20 minutes, or until the outside is crispy and deeply colored. Remove from oven. Drain and reserve bacon fat. Cut slices into ¼-inch lardons (perpendicular to the slice length). Reserve lardons.

Rinse Kalettes. Trim base of stalk of any browning, and remove any outer leaves that are broken or brown. Place Kalettes in a large, metal mixing bowl.

Blanch the French beans and pearl onions. Cut beans lengthwise and onions in half, parallel to the root to display the rings. Add pomegranate arils, clementines, French beans, and pearl onions to the Kalettes.

Combine apple cider, cider vinegar, Dijon, honey, sea salt, and pepper in a metal mixing bowl. While whisking, drizzle in grapeseed oil to emulsify. In a medium saucepan, heat ½ cup of reserved bacon fat. Add shallots, and sauté for 2 minutes. Add lardons, and sauté for an additional 2 minutes. Pour dressing into pan, and bring to a boil. Remove from heat.

TO SERVE

Preheat oven to 375° F. Heat pork in the oven for 15 minutes. Toss Kalette salad with warm bacon cider vinaigrette to coat. Spoon warm grits onto plates. Place pork half on grits, and drizzle generously with pomegranate gastrique. Arrange salad on plate, garnish, and enjoy!

Chef Sean Harrison, Chef Ryan Rudnick, and Chef Walter Slawski

Rabbi Jake Rubin Col '02

Originally from Richmond, Virginia, Rabbi Jake Rubin holds a B.A. in religious studies from the University of Virginia. In 2009, he received his rabbinic ordination from the Reconstructionist Rabbinical College (RRC), from which he also graduated with a Master of Arts in Hebrew letters.

While a student at RRC, he served as the Jewish student advisor at Swarthmore College, an affiliate of Hillel of Greater Philadelphia. He also worked as a chaplain for Jewish Family and Children's Service of Greater Philadelphia and as an educator and student rabbi for a number of congregations during his time at RRC. Prior to rabbinical school, he was a fellow for PANIM, the Institute for Jewish Leadership and Values.

Rabbi Jake has been the executive director of the Brody Jewish Center at the University of Virginia since 2009. During his tenure, he has served as the president of United Ministries at UVA, as a coach for new Hillel directors, and as a member of Hillel International's Directors Cabinet. He was awarded the prestigious Cohen Fellowship, as well as the Richard M. Joel Exemplar of Excellence award for his contributions to the Hillel movement.

Rabbi Jake, through the Brody Jewish Center and Hillel, strives to make Judaism meaningful and relevant for Jewish students at the University. By creating a vibrant and welcoming community, Hillel seeks to create a home away from home for Jewish students at UVA. The Brody Jewish Center develops relationships, communities, and opportunities that empower Jewish students to take ownership of their Jewish identities.

In his spare time, Rabbi Jake enjoys spending time with his family, reading, and going to concerts. He lives in Charlottesville with his wife, Lindsay, and their children, Sophie, Jonah, and Caleb.

The following recipe has won the Brody Jewish Center's Brisket Cook-Off multiple times.

 The UVA chapter of Challah for Hunger is one of the most successful chapters, bringing together student volunteers to raise money and awareness for hunger relief. The UVA chapter sells challah on the Lawn and at Congregation Beth Israel, donating all proceeds.

Prize-Winning Brisket

1 3–5-pound beef brisket
8 tablespoons dried onion soup mix
6 tablespoons light brown sugar, firmly packed
1 (12 ounces) bottle of barbecue sauce
1–1¼ cups of water, depending on desired thickness
Olive oil, enough to cover the bottom of a frying pan

Preheat oven to 250°F.

Trim excess fat from the brisket. Mix onion soup mix and brown sugar together and divide in half. Sprinkle half of this mixture evenly on both sides of the brisket.

Heat the olive oil in the frying pan, and brown the brisket on all sides (a couple of minutes at most on each side).

Take the second half of the onion soup mix and brown sugar mixture and sprinkle each side of the brisket again. Place brisket into roasting pan, fat side up. Mix the barbecue sauce with water, and pour over brisket. Cover pan tightly with aluminum foil.

Place in oven. Turn the brisket over every hour or so. Bake until fork tender. Depending on the size of your brisket, it may take 5 hours, or more or less.

Let the brisket cool before cutting. Place the pieces back in the sauce and chill. Reheat when ready to serve.

Ron Hutchins

VICE PRESIDENT FOR INFORMATION TECHNOLOGY

Ron Hutchins joined the University of Virginia as Vice President for Information Technology in August 2015. During his first year at UVA, Ron found many opportunities to stretch his food interests around the Charlottesville area.

Between great restaurants, the City Market on Saturday mornings, wonderful local food stores, and the Morven Kitchen Garden CSA shares, Ron has found a regional food haven that soothes the palate and challenges the inner foodie to be more and more creative. The Charlottesville area has provided Ron with an opportunity to learn and grow (in more ways than one) in food culture. As a most welcome addition, the local wines are always a treat!

Sauces are one of the gifts of French cuisine, and Beaucaire Chicken makes use of one of the simplest sauces: a white wine and cream sauce. This dish was created in Beaucaire, France, in Provence, from whatever was in the refrigerator at the time. Ron enjoyed it so much and has come to depend on its flavor and simplicity on a somewhat regular basis.

The following dish works well with legs and thighs or breasts. The flavor needs some hearty pasta to stick to. Bowties are good, but the best is a rustic, homemade fettuccini or tagliatelle. There's nothing quite as good as rolling out pasta dough, wrapping it around a rolling pin, and cutting it into ribbons that are rough and thick to hold onto this sauce. The tomatoes and avocados don't need cooking, just bringing up to temperature, so don't overcook!

Beaucaire Chicken

2–4 chicken legs/thighs (breasts are okay, too)
2–4 tablespoons olive oil, depending on how much
 chicken you're using
2–4 tablespoons butter
6 cloves garlic, smashed and finely chopped
1 shallot, finely chopped
1 small white onion, chopped small
¼–½ cup white wine
½–1 cup heavy cream
¼ cup shredded Parmigiano
2 tomatoes, cut in ½-inch cubes
½ to 1 avocado, roughly sliced
10 basil leaves, medium chopped

Preheat the oven to 375°F.

Heat the olive oil in an oven-safe pan on the stovetop.
Sauté the chicken pieces for 30 minutes, turning once.
Once browned on both sides, place the pan in the oven
for 25 minutes, until chicken is just barely done. Take the
chicken out of the pan, but leave the remains in the skillet
for the sauce. After chicken cools, pull from the bones,
cut up a bit, and set aside.

In the oil left in the pan, add the butter, and put back on
the stovetop on medium heat. After the butter melts, add
the garlic and cook until aroma appears. Add the shallots
and onion, and cook until transparent. Then add the white
wine and cook until reduced to nearly the original amount
of liquid. Add cream and cook 1 minute. Add Parmigiano,
and stir to incorporate and thicken. Add the chicken and
heat through, stirring. Stir in the tomatoes and avocado,
and just heat through. Add the basil and stir for 1 minute.
Remove from heat and serve over freshly cooked tagliatelle pasta (preferably rustic homemade pasta).

Enjoy!

Chef Tanya Holland Col '87

EXECUTIVE CHEF AND OWNER OF
BROWN SUGAR KITCHEN AND B-SIDE BBQ

Tanya Holland is the executive chef and owner of Brown Sugar Kitchen and B-Side BBQ in Oakland, California. With her father from Virginia and her mother from Louisiana, Tanya grew up experiencing the food and culture of those regions. Now, her restaurants reflect the regional cuisine of the South, particularly the soul food of African Americans whose roots lie there.

The author of *New Soul Cooking: Updating a Cuisine Rich in Flavor and Tradition* (Stewart, Tabori, and Chang, 2003) and *Brown Sugar Kitchen: New-Style, Down-Home Recipes from Sweet West Oakland* (Chronicle Books, 2014), Tanya is also known for her role as a host and expert on soul food for the *Melting Pot* series on the Food Network and the Cooking Channel.

Before becoming a chef, Tanya thought she wanted to be an engineer. But when she wasn't admitted to UVA's School of Engineering, she enrolled in the College of Arts and Sciences instead. She discovered that she excelled in languages and decided to major in Slavic languages and literature. Tanya enjoyed the language, linguistics, and culture, but most of all, she enjoyed the freedom her new major allowed. Suddenly, she had time to enjoy her favorite extracurricular activities: working in restaurants, dining in restaurants, hosting dinner parties, and experimenting with food.

Tanya found herself dining out more as she moved farther away from Grounds. Her favorite places in Charlottesville were the Virginian and Eastern Standard on the Downtown Mall. They were quite a contrast. She liked the rustic elegance and comfort of the Virginian and the edgy sophistication of Eastern Standard. She continues to seek similar experiences in dining and in her creation of food and environment. There was definitely a part of her that thought, *I'd like to do this one day—create an establishment that people want to hang out in over and over again. It's better than a party...it's a way of life.*

And not to leave her college major behind, Tanya's culinary experience and familiarity with the Slavic culture collided when the U.S. State Department asked her to be a culinary diplomat to Kazakhstan. She is sharing some of the recipes she created inspired by her time there. Nostrovia!

Summer Rice Salad

(serves 6)

2 cups long-grain white rice, uncooked
1 ear of corn, kernels removed
1 small zucchini, diced
1 bunch thin asparagus, cut into 1-inch pieces
1 cup slivered almonds
¼ cup thinly sliced basil
¼ cup thinly sliced mint
¼ cup chopped parsley
⅓ cup diced dill pickles
½ cup dried currants

Dressing

2 garlic cloves, grated on a microplane
½ teaspoon fine sea salt
1 tablespoon apple cider vinegar
¼ cup extra-virgin olive oil

Cook rice according to package instructions; do not over-cook. Cool slightly.

Toss cooled rice with all salad ingredients.

In a small bowl, whisk together salad dressing ingredients. Dress the rice mixture while warm, so dressing is absorbed.

Serve warm, cold, or at room temperature.

Lamb Kebabs

Lamb Kebabs with Tomato and Plum Salad

(serves 4)

Kebabs
1 pound boneless leg of lamb, cut into
    1-inch cubes
¾ teaspoon fine sea salt, divided
¼ teaspoon cayenne pepper
½ teaspoon caraway seeds
1 teaspoon ground cumin
1 cinnamon stick
2 cloves garlic, smashed
Zest and juice of 1 lemon
1 tablespoon chopped fresh oregano
¼ cup thinly sliced mint
½ cup thinly sliced basil
½ cup chopped parsley
¾ cup extra-virgin olive oil

Salad
2 large tomatoes, cut into ½-inch dice
3 plums, cut into ½-inch dice
½ teaspoon fine sea salt
2 tablespoons extra-virgin olive oil

Place lamb, ¼ teaspoon salt, cayenne, caraway seeds, cumin, cinnamon stick, and garlic in a large, resealable plastic bag.

In a small bowl, combine lemon zest, juice, herbs, olive oil, and remaining salt. Dump half the herb sauce into the lamb mixture. Reserve the remaining sauce for garnish and dipping. Seal plastic bag, removing all air, and refrigerate at least 1 hour and up to 12 hours.

To create the salad, combine all ingredients in a large bowl and toss. Cover the salad, and refrigerate while the lamb is marinating. This will develop and deepen the flavors.

Preheat a grill to medium-high.

Skewer lamb cubes, placing about 4 pieces of lamb per skewer. Grill each skewer for 2–3 minutes per side for medium rare.

Serve kebabs with additional herb sauce and alongside tomato plum salad.

When Food and Wine *magazine asked Chef Tanya Holland what dish tells her story, there was only one answer—shrimp and grits. Grits are a large part of her heritage, so Tanya feels a special connection to the dish. Her recipe also showcases a French technique—sauté—which speaks to her training at La Varenne.*

This recipe for Creole Shrimp and Grits is from her cookbook Brown Sugar Kitchen: New-Style, Down-Home Recipes from Sweet West Oakland.

Creole Shrimp & Grits

(serves 4)

2 tablespoons vegetable oil
¼ cup diced green bell pepper
¼ cup diced red bell pepper
3 green onions, white and green parts, thinly sliced
2 garlic cloves, minced
2 teaspoons Creole Spice Mix *(See recipe)*
1½ pounds medium shrimp, peeled and deveined
¾ cup Creole Sauce *(See recipe)*
¼ cup heavy cream
2 tablespoons unsalted butter
5 ounces baby spinach leaves
2 teaspoons fresh lemon juice
White cheddar grits *(See recipe)* for serving

In a large sauté pan, heat the oil over medium heat until shimmering.

Add the green and red bell peppers, green onions, garlic, and the Creole Spice Mix, and cook until the vegetables are softened, about 5 minutes. Add the shrimp and sear just until opaque, turning once, about 2 minutes. Stir in the Creole Sauce, cream, and butter, and bring to a simmer. Add the spinach, a handful at a time, stirring to wilt and coat with sauce. Once all the spinach has been added, remove the pan from the heat and stir in the lemon juice. Serve immediately over the grits.

Creole Spice Mix

(yields about 1½ cups)

3 tablespoons kosher salt
3 tablespoons herbes de Provence
3 tablespoons ground cumin
⅓ cup cayenne pepper
¼ cup freshly ground black pepper
¼ cup sweet paprika

In a small bowl, stir together the salt, herbes de Provence, cumin, cayenne, black pepper, and paprika until thoroughly combined.

(To make ahead, store in an airtight container for up to 6 months.)

Creole Sauce

(yields about 1 cup)

1 tablespoon unsalted butter
2 green onions, white parts only, chopped
1 teaspoon minced garlic
1 (12 ounces) bottle wheat beer,
    such as Hefeweizen
¾ cup Worcestershire sauce

In a medium saucepan, melt the butter over low heat. Add the green onions and garlic, and cook until softened, about 5 minutes. Add the beer and Worcestershire sauce and increase the heat to medium-high. Bring to a boil, reduce to a simmer, and cook until thick and syrupy and reduced to about 1 cup, 15–20 minutes. Remove from heat and let cool.

(To make ahead, refrigerate sauce in an airtight container for up to 1 week.)

White Cheddar Grits

(serves 4)

2¾ cups water
2⅔ cups quick-cooking grits
2 tablespoons heavy cream
2 tablespoons unsalted butter
4 ounces sharp white cheddar cheese, grated
1½ teaspoons kosher salt
Pinch of white pepper

In a medium saucepan, bring the water to a boil. Whisk in the grits, reduce to a simmer, and cook, stirring constantly, until the grits are fully cooked and thick like mush, about 4 minutes. Stir in the cream, butter, cheese, salt, and white pepper.

Cover and keep warm over very low heat until serving.

Sarah Lanzman

CHEF AND CO-OWNER OF BLISS POINT FARM
BLISSPOINTFARM.COM

Sarah Lanzman has been a professional chef for over thirty years. For sixteen years, she and her husband ran their own company, Lorelei Caterers, in Charlottesville for which she won several awards. She has catered for numerous events at the University of Virginia, including a reception for Julian Bond when he became Board Chairman of the NAACP in 1998.

Most recently, Sarah was the executive chef and Director of Food Services at the Virginia Center for the Creative Arts in Amherst, a residential artists' and writers' retreat center. Sarah is also a personal chef, specializing in organic, whole foods with gluten-free and vegan options. She is a certified integrative nutrition consultant (CNC) and health coach, as well as a certified natural health professional (CNHP). She has taught healthy cooking classes, as well as holistic wellness workshops geared toward specific illnesses. She has had recipes and articles published in many magazines and newspapers and communicates her social activism through her cooking and the choices she makes about her mission, events, and people she serves.

Sarah has a holistic approach to health and cooking. Flavor in her dishes reflects the local, natural, and organic foods she uses in her recipes. Sarah is building Bliss Point Farm, just outside of Charlottesville, with her husband, Reimer Brodersen. They practice sustainable, biological farming, producing tree fruit, vegetables, herbs, and flowers. They are dedicated to sustainable living practices and environmental, nutritional, and cooking education.

Bliss Point Farm and Retreat Center is in a converted historical country store, built in 1891 on twelve beautiful acres in the Blue Ridge Mountains of central Virginia. At Bliss Point Farm, you will be able to experience the Blue Ridge Mountains at their B&B, eat nutritious organic and local foods, receive personalized health consultations, take healthy therapeutic cooking classes, and attend workshops.

Caribbean Chicken

Caribbean Chicken Breast Rolls Stuffed with Fresh
Mango Coconut, Curry, and Lime

(serves 8 as a main course)

2 large, fresh, ripe mangoes, pitted and cut into ¼-inch pieces
1 tablespoon cornstarch
1 tablespoon lime juice
1 tablespoon dark brown sugar
½ cup unsweetened coconut, shredded
½ cup scallions (green onions), finely chopped
2 tablespoons chopped fresh cilantro and some for garnishing
1 tablespoon grated fresh ginger
1 tablespoon mild curry powder
1 teaspoon ground allspice
⅛ teaspoon cayenne pepper
8 split, boneless chicken breasts with skin on
2 tablespoons coconut oil, melted
2 tablespoons coconut oil for coating baking pan
Salt to taste

In a medium bowl, combine the mangoes, cornstarch, lime juice, brown sugar, shredded coconut, scallions, cilantro, and spices. Set aside.

Coat a rimmed metal baking sheet with the coconut oil. Set aside.

Preheat oven to 375°F.

Place a chicken breast on a clean surface, skin side up. Trim away any excess fat. Loosen the skin from one side of the breast. Stuff about ½ cup of the filling under the skin. Tuck the skin and meat under to form an even dome shape. Place the stuffed breasts onto the sheet pan. Coat the chicken breast with the melted coconut oil, and lightly salt the top.

Bake until golden brown, about 20 minutes. Be careful not to overcook, as chicken can dry out.

Cool slightly before serving. If you are going to slice into hors d'oeuvres, let cool a little longer. Arrange on platters, and garnish with cilantro.

Striped Bass Fillet

Striped Bass Fillet with an Albemarle Pippin Coulis

(serves 6)

6 (6 ounces) striped bass fillets (same as rockfish), with skin
½ cup grapeseed oil
6 Albemarle Pippin apples, peeled, cored, and quartered
1 tablespoon plus 1 teaspoon unsalted butter
¼ cup agave nectar
2 teaspoons ground cinnamon
½ teaspoon ground mace
1½ teaspoons fresh lemon juice
Zest of 1 organic lemon
1 tablespoon plus 1 teaspoon brandy
1 tablespoon water
Salt and black pepper to taste

Preheat oven to 450°F. Oil a shallow baking pan.

Pat fish dry with paper towels. Score skin in several places with a thin, sharp knife to prevent fish from curling; do not cut through flesh. Season lightly on all sides with salt and pepper.

Heat oil in a heavy-bottom, large frying pan over medium-high heat until hot but not smoking. Add fish fillets, skin side down, in batches. Sear until skin is golden brown and crisp, 3–4 minutes per batch (fish will not be fully cooked). Transfer to oiled baking pan, turning fish skin side up. Roast fish in oven, uncovered, until just cooked through, 7–8 minutes.

To make the coulis to drizzle over the cooked fish, place the apples in a heavy-bottomed saucepan. Add butter, agave nectar, cinnamon, mace, lemon juice, zest, brandy, and water. Cover and simmer over low heat, stirring occasionally, until fork pierces through the apples easily. Cool slightly and then process in a blender or food processor until totally smooth and free of lumps. Pour into a squeeze bottle.

The coulis can be made one day ahead, covered, and refrigerated. To serve, drizzle over the fish and serve hot.

Laura Brown Col '10

DIRECTOR OF COMMUNICATIONS
AND MARKETING, LOCAL FOOD HUB

Growing up in Charlottesville, Laura Brown has long felt a strong connection to food and farming. From visiting the City Market on the weekends to gardening and cooking at home with her family, nutritious food and healthy eating have always been a focal point. She has always appreciated knowing where her food comes from and values the stories behind the farm families that feed her community.

While an undergraduate at UVA studying foreign affairs, Laura discovered a career path in her passion for local food systems. She took several courses in food politics and food system planning. After graduation, she landed a job with the U.S. Department of Agriculture (USDA) in Washington, D.C., thanks to a fellow UVA alum who was also employed there. Laura worked at the USDA for four years, serving in the Office of Congressional Relations, the primary liaison between the USDA and Congress, the Farm and Foreign Agricultural Services, and finally, with the National Farm to School Program, where she further honed her career aspirations. She supported efforts to increase access to local food and to incorporate food and farming education in school systems across the country. Laura also helped administer a $5 million grant program.

While she found the work at the USDA rewarding and fascinating, she missed her hometown of Charlottesville and wanted to support local food efforts in her own community. Local Food Hub, a nonprofit organization that partners with Virginia farmers to increase community access to local food, began in Charlottesville while Laura was at UVA and had always been of interest to her.

In 2014, Local Food Hub had a communications and marketing need, just when she was ready to move back home. Two years later, Laura is loving life in Hooville with her longtime boyfriend and their two dogs in what they feel is one of—if not—the best towns for local food, culture, and outdoor activities. They are avid runners, hikers, and triathletes. They enjoy eating their way around town and meeting the farm families who feed the community. Laura encourages people everywhere to shop at their local farmers' market or natural foods store for fresh, seasonal items and to support small family farms in their community.

Veggie Tacos

Veggie Tacos with Easy Homemade Salsa

(serves 4)

2 pounds tomatoes (Campari work great, but any will do.)
1–3 jalapeño peppers (Use more or less, depending on how spicy you like salsa.)
2–3 garlic cloves
1 summer squash
1 zucchini squash
1 medium onion
Olive oil
1 bunch cilantro
12 corn tortillas
Feta cheese
Yogurt or sour cream for topping

Slice the tomatoes in half if they are small or quarters if they are large. Slice the jalapeños in half, and remove the stems. Place tomatoes, jalapeños, and garlic cloves on a broiler pan or baking sheet and broil on high for 5–20 minutes (depending on the strength of your broiler) until the veggies start to brown. Remove from the oven. Let cool.

Dice the squash, zucchini, and onion. Put some olive oil in a cast-iron skillet or saucepan and turn on medium heat. Add the squash, zucchini, and onion, and cook until they are crisp, not mushy, and the onion browns a bit, about 10–15 minutes.

Put the cooled tomato, jalapeños, and garlic cloves into a food processor or blender, and puree to your desired consistency. You may add some water if you prefer a thinner salsa.

Chop the cilantro and place in a bowl.

Assemble your tacos with the squash, zucchini, and onion added first. Top with salsa, cilantro, feta cheese, and yogurt or sour cream.

Francesca Fiorani

PROFESSOR OF ART HISTORY AND ASSOCIATE DEAN FOR THE ARTS AND HUMANITIES IN THE COLLEGE AND GRADUATE SCHOOL OF ARTS AND SCIENCES

Francesca Fiorani is Professor of Art History and Associate Dean for the Arts and Humanities in the College and Graduate School of Arts and Sciences. Born and raised in Rome, she studied art history at the University of Rome "La Sapienza," specializing in the art of the Renaissance. She is an expert on the relationship between art and science and, in addition to writing on great Renaissance artists like Leonardo da Vinci, she is interested in a wide variety of less usual images, such scientific images, maps, geometrical diagrams, sky charts, and blueprints for mechanical tools.

Her academic and professional career developed in Europe, the US, and the Middle East, and she has lived and conducted research in Rome, Berlin, London, Paris, Tel Aviv, Berkeley, and New York, among other places. One of her books, *The Marvel of Maps. Art, Cartography and Politics in Renaissance Italy* (Yale University Press, 2005) was a runner-up for the Premio Salimbeni per la Storia e la Critica d'Arte, a book prize awarded by the president of Italy. She has also embraced advanced technology in the study of the arts and the humanities, and working together with computer engineers, programmers, librarians, and scholars, she has created an internationally-renowned digital publication titled *Leonardo da Vinci and His Treatise on Painting*. Her scholarly work has been recognized by numerous foundations and granting agencies, including the John Simon Guggenheim Memorial Foundation, the American Council for the Learned Societies, the Harvard Center for Renaissance Studies at Villa I Tatti, the Getty Center, the National Endowment for the Humanities, the Folger Institute, and the Warburg Institute.

She has traveled extensively throughout her life especially in Africa, the Middle East, Europe, and the Mediterranean, and arrived in Charlottesville about twenty years ago for what she thought was a brief visit. She stayed because of the University and the opportunities it offered to pursue her scholarship. Although she continues to travel often, at times for extended periods of time, Charlottesville is her new hometown. Her two children were born at the UVA hospital; one works in New York, the other is a fourth year economics major at the University.

Wherever she goes, she is curious about local culinary traditions and visits vegetable markets and local restaurants. Eating around a table with family and friends for lunch and dinner was part and parcel of her growing up in Italy, and she has maintained this tradition with her own family and friends.

A talented cook, she has tried many different recipes from different world regions. At the end, though, it is the Mediterranean cuisine of her childhood that she always goes back to and that she really knows how to cook. Her pasta dishes and seafood entrees have become legendary among her friends. She does not cook with butter or margarine, just with extra-virgin olive oil. She prefers simple recipes based on very few ingredients of high quality and selects locally grown vegetables and fruits, wild-caught seafood, and fresh herbs. Her recipe for this book is a quick, light, and *gustoso* summer dish that can be prepared in just a few minutes.

Pasta with Cherry Tomatoes and Herbs

(serves 4)

1 pound spaghetti or linguini: it is best to select high-quality pasta
    by an Italian pasta maker
Salt to taste
½ cup extra-virgin olive oil (cold press is better)
2 large garlic cloves
3 pints organic or locally grown cherry tomatoes
½ cup chopped fresh basil
¼ cup chopped parsley
¼ cup chopped sage
⅕ cup fresh oregano

As is typical for recipes as simple as this one, ingredients may vary a little. Some may choose to add a few more cherry tomatoes, others may wish to switch the quantities of oregano and basil, others still may prefer to eliminate sage.

Cut cherry tomatoes in half and clean garlic cloves.

Heat extra-virgin olive oil in large nonstick saucepan over medium-high. Add garlic cloves to saucepan, cook until they become brownish and then remove from saucepan.

Add cherry tomatoes to saucepan, spreading them in the pan. Let them cook for 5–10 minutes, depending on how big they are. Do not touch or turn the tomatoes until they get a little brownish on one side. If needed shake the saucepan gently to avoid having them to the bottom. Add herbs but keep half of the basil. Add salt.

Bring to boil a large pot of water. Add salt. Cook pasta until al dente.

Drain pasta and toss it in saucepan with cherry tomatoes and herbs. Stir pasta, cherry tomatoes, and herbs, and cook for about 1 minute.

Toss in large serving bowl—better to use a shallow serving bowl than a deep one as the tomatoes tend to converge to the bottom. Sprinkle the remaining basil. Serve and enjoy.

Ashley East Col '02

CHEF AND OWNER OF DINNER AT HOME (DaH) CATERING

Ashley East, owner of Dinner at Home Catering in Charlottesville, developed a love for food and cooking at a young age and was working in restaurants by the time she was fourteen. Ashley must have picked up some culinary vibes from her late grandfather, Frank J. Hightower, whose Cellar Restaurant in Oklahoma City was once the Southwest's go-to place for haute cuisine. Drawing inspiration from master chefs Julia Child and James Beard, Hightower offered not only memorable dining experiences but also sponsored cooking classes for food lovers who were serious about the art of fine dining.

Ashley studied and played field hockey at Colgate University for two years before finding her true home at UVA in the fall of 2000. While she holds a Bachelor of Arts in economics, her passion has always been firmly planted in the culinary world. She began working at the Ivy Inn as a prep cook shortly after moving to Charlottesville. In 2001, she attended Cookery at the Grange in Somerset, England, to further her skills.

In 2003, Ashley founded Dinner at Home (DaH) as a personal chef and caterer. Over the years, she worked at local restaurants, such as the Clifton Inn, and taught cooking classes. While working with local chefs Angelo Vangelopoulos and Tucker Yoder, she took a keen interest in farm-to-table fare and made a commitment to source ingredients locally whenever possible. While DaH continues to grow, Ashley is still devoted to the personal touch she imagined from the start. But large events, such as weddings, make up most of the calendar.

Balancing work and motherhood is her hardest but most rewarding challenge to date. On days off, she can be found baking with her son, Isaac, and riding her bike. When cooking for her family, Ashley loves to make braised chicken, panzanella, and anything with fresh fish.

Trout Fillets

Trout Fillets with Butternut Squash-Apple-Bacon Hash and Microgreens Salad

(serves 4 as an appetizer or small main)

Microgreen Salad
4 ounces microgreens (such as baby tatsoi
    or arugula), washed
½ clove garlic, minced
1 teaspoon Dijon mustard
2 tablespoons apple cider vinegar
1 teaspoon honey
¼ cup extra-virgin olive oil
Pinch of salt

Hash
1 cup butternut squash, diced
1 tart apple (such as Pink Lady), diced
2 slices bacon, minced
¼ cup yellow onion, minced
1 clove garlic, minced
2 teaspoons fresh thyme, minced
1 teaspoon maple syrup
1 teaspoon whole-grain mustard
Pinch of cayenne
Salt and pepper to taste

Trout
¼ cup fine polenta (for dusting)
1 ounce unsalted butter
2 tablespoons extra-virgin olive oil
Salt and pepper to taste

To prepare dressing, whisk all ingredients in a small bowl or shake in a jar. Set aside.

To prepare hash, blanch the butternut squash in boiling water for 4 minutes, drain, and put in ice water bath. In a sauté pan, place squash, apple, bacon, onion, and garlic. Sauté until squash and apple are fork tender. Stir in thyme, maple syrup, whole-grain mustard, and a pinch of cayenne. Season with salt and pepper to taste. Set aside while cooking fish.

Season trout with salt and pepper on each side and dust with polenta. Heat a sauté pan to medium-high heat, add butter and oil. When fats are hot, add fish and cook on each side about 2–3 minutes until crispy on each side and cooked through.

Meanwhile, toss greens with dressing.

Transfer fish to plates, and top with hash. Add a small salad to each plate.

Ed Hardy Col '02

BACON N' EDS FOOD TRUCK

Ed Hardy had plenty of universities to choose from but decided to enroll at the UVA for one reason: the infamous Virginia Pep Band. Reflecting on his undergraduate years, he describes a "perfect storm" of pressures to jump into the culinary field. Along with the rise of the Food Network and celebrity chefs, the Pep Band was also full of culinary experimenters.

During his extended undergraduate years in Charlottesville, Hardy paid for tuition with jobs at Southern Culture and eventually became executive chef at the Virginian. After a brief stint in Virginia politics and a Capitol Hill internship, he returned to cooking and enrolled at the prestigious French Culinary Institute in New York City. While in New York, much of his time was spent working with *Top Chef* master Marcus Samuelsson. With Chef Samuelsson, Ed opened and helped lead the acclaimed restaurants Red Rooster and American Table

at Lincoln Center. Chef Ed began his stint with Chef Samuelsson at Aquavit NYC, where he started on the line. He also spent time as sous chef at the Modern/MoMA Café and as a stagiaire at the legacy restaurant Gramercy Tavern.

After moving to the D.C. area in 2012, Ed was named executive chef of the critically acclaimed Bistro Vivant in McLean, Virginia, and then later as chef and partner at Quench in Rockville, Maryland, which was named best new restaurant.

After Quench was sold, Hardy decided that it was time to strike out on his own. Telling edgy jokes in front of thousands of people with the Pep Band gave Chef Hardy great practice and the confidence necessary for cooking on the Food Network, where he has already appeared on two cooking competitions and is scheduled to appear in more.

Low Country Cuban Press

(yields 5–6 sandwiches)

2 pounds pork belly, trimmed
1 ounce pink curing salt
1 cup brown sugar
1 cup kosher salt
2 tablespoons cumin
2 tablespoons chili powder
2 tablespoons mustard seeds
2 tablespoons smoked paprika
1 beer (American IPA, if possible)
5–6 sub rolls
Butter
12–14 slices Grayson Cheese from Meadow Creek Dairy (or Swiss cheese or provolone)
1 pound real country ham (or Surryano or similar)
Deli mustard
Pickled watermelon rind or dill pickles

Slice pork belly into ½-inch slices. Make the cure/rub, combine the curing salt, brown sugar, salt, cumin, chili powder, and mustard seeds in a small bowl. Cover the pork belly liberally with the cure/rub. Cover and refrigerate for 3–4 hours.

Preheat oven to 300°F. Then braise in a covered pan with beer (IPA, if possible) for 3½ hours.

To finish the sandwiches, brush the outside of the rolls with butter. Layer cheese, ham, pork belly, pickles, and mustard inside, and close the sandwich. Put into a hot pan and press down with hot cast iron skillet on top until cheese has melted and the outside is golden brown.

Jody Kielbasa

VICE PROVOST FOR THE ARTS

Jody Kielbasa moved to Charlottesville with his wife, Helen, and three children, Camille, Luke, and Juliet, in 2009 to direct the Virginia Film Festival. Jody was the founding director of the Sarasota Film Festival. He spent ten years expanding it to include the Sarasota Film Festival Outreach and Education Program. Jody was pleased to accept the opportunity to come to Virginia to direct a film festival at the center of such an acclaimed academic institution.

In 2013, he was appointed Vice Provost for the Arts, responsible for planning for the arts in consultation with the Arts Advisory Committee, participating in fundraising initiatives, and initiating and coordinating cross-disciplinary collaborations. He continues to serve as the director of the film festival.

Jody's grandparents emigrated from Poland at the beginning of the twentieth century. His parents were born in New England and grew up during the Great Depression in a Polish community. His father was a Marine in WWII, serving as a cook in the Pacific Theater.

When Jody was a boy, his parents often prepared some of the simpler foods that were Polish staples. Kielbasa, pierogis, and kapusta were among his favorites. This kapusta recipe, a wonderful, sweet cabbage, is one of several fillings common to pierogis. Potatoes, cheese, and blueberries are equally common.

Pierogi

Pierogi Stuffed with Kapusta

½ cup of milk
1 tablespoon butter, melted in milk
½ cup of water
2 large eggs
4 cups of flour
1 small cabbage, 2–2½ pounds
1 large jar of sauerkraut
½ pound of salt pork
3–4 onions, finely chopped
Butter

To make the pierogi dough, warm the milk and melt the butter into it. Add the ½ cup of water and beat the eggs into the mixture. Gradually add the 4 cups of flour, mixing with a spatula. Continue adding the flour until a batter-like mixture forms. Sprinkle flour onto the board, and knead until it no longer sticks to your hands or the board, adding more flour if necessary. Divide the dough, and roll into a thin layer to form into the pierogi dumplings. *(Chef's Note: Let the pierogi dough rest before rolling.)*

To make the kapusta, finely chop the cabbage. Drain the sauerkraut in a strainer, saving the juice for later. Rinse the sauerkraut and chop. Combine the cabbage and the sauerkraut, and boil for 15 minutes.

Finely chop the salt pork. Mix with the onions, and sauté with butter over low heat until the pork is lightly crisped. *(Chef's Note: Soak the salt pork in water to release some salt, at least an hour.)*

Strain the cabbage and sauerkraut, add the onions and salt pork, ¼ cup of the reserved sauerkraut juice, and a tablespoon of butter. Continue to sauté for another 10–15 minutes and then cool.

Cut the dough into circles. Add a tablespoon or so of kapusta, fold the dough over, and close.

Boil the pierogi for 10 minutes. Remove from water and cool. After cooling, lightly fry the pierogi in butter until golden brown. Serve with a side of kapusta, kielbasa sausage, beets, and a dollop of sour cream.

Kay Pfaltz Col '83

FOUNDER OF BASIC NECESSITIES

Rosie Gantt, Sallie Justice, and Kay Pfaltz, co-owners of Basic Necessities

Kay Pfaltz spent more than ten years working and living in Paris, and she credits UVA with getting her there. Although not in the way one might expect...

As a second year student, Kay was struggling through French 201 when her teacher informed the class that they could fulfill their requirement with three weeks in Paris...in the dead of winter. The struggling student boarded a plane for the City of Light and fell in love. There was the French capital, with its abundance of art, tree-lined boulevards, narrow cobblestone streets, and the French outlook on life. But above all, there was the food. Bistros, brasseries, haute cuisine, nouvelle cuisine, bakeries, cheese shops, markets. The three weeks changed Kay's life.

After graduating and a stint at Chemical Bank in Manhattan, Kay realized her heart belonged in Paris. In her new adoptive city, she found her passion in literature and philosophy, leaving her beloved city only to complete an M.A. and later a Ph.D. in literature at King's College, University of London. It was also in Paris that she developed a love of food—a love that would take her around the world. Hers was a journey to understand different cultures through their cuisines.

After spending many long hours trying to perfect the French baguette—and failing—she decided to do something about it. In 1997, she opened **Basic Necessities,** a small restaurant and gourmet shop, to offer locals the "basic necessities" of life: good wine, bread, cheese, and chocolate.

Today, Kay spends her time teaching wine tasting and writing as a columnist, essayist, and author of five books. Her favorite book is her first, *Lauren's Story: An American Dog in Paris*, which chronicles her life in Paris, dining out in the city's best restaurants, with a little stray beagle from Virginia. All profits from her books go to animal rescue, her other passion.

The little restaurant that was born of necessity has now evolved into a necessity for many faithful customers. Basic Necessities specializes in local, organic, and seasonal produce, just as Kay's wine selection centers around small-production, organic, and biodynamic wines. And mostly French, *bien sûr*.

Wild Green Pie is a favorite of Basic Necessities' customers and staff. Sallie Justice, chef and co-owner, embellished the recipe. Not only does it afford the opportunity to pick fresh, local greens, but it is also healthy and delicious!

Basic Necessities'
Wild Green Pie

(serves 8–10)

8 ounces fresh spinach
8 ounces mixed greens, such as sorrel, dandelions, mustard
    greens, watercress, arugula, kale, and chard
1 cup water
¼ cup olive oil
1 leek, minced
½ cup sliced scallions (green onions)
½ teaspoon minced fresh hot green or red pepper
¾ cup crumbled feta cheese
¾ cup (approximately 3 ounces) grated pecorino or Parmesan
    cheese
1 large egg
½ cup chopped fresh dill weed
½ cup chopped fennel fronds or finely minced fennel bulb
½ cup golden raisins
10–12 filo sheets
Salt to taste
Olive oil

Rinse and coarsely chop the spinach and mixed greens. Heat the water in a skillet, and add half the greens. Cook for 5 minutes, or until wilted and tender. Stir in remaining greens. Cook covered, until all the greens are wilted. Drain, pressing to remove any excess water. Coarsely chop the greens.

Heat 2 tablespoons of the olive oil in a large skillet. Add the leek and scallions, and sauté until tender. Add the remaining 2 tablespoons olive oil, chopped greens, and hot pepper. Cook for 3 minutes. Remove from the heat and cool briefly. Stir in the feta cheese, pecorino or Parmesan cheese, egg, dill, fennel, and raisins and mix well. Season with salt.

Preheat the oven to 375°F. Brush a 12-inch round baking dish with olive oil. Layer the phyllo sheets in the baking dish, brushing each sheet with olive oil and allowing a 1- to 2-inch overhang. Spread the greens mixture evenly over the filo, pressing it down with a spoon. Crimp the phyllo above the edge. Bake for 35–45 minutes, or until phyllo is golden brown.

Pat Pitts, Gordon Sutton, and Taylor Sutton

FOOD SERVICE MANAGER OF BELLAIR MARKET, FAMILY OWNERS OF THE TIGER FUEL COMPANY

Bellair Market is a one-stop shop operation and has been for over twenty-five years. And that's what makes it so appealing. You can get gas, espresso, a fresh gourmet sub, or poached salmon—with a bottle of local wine! The market's goal is to serve fresh, quality food as quickly as possible.

Pat's journey to Bellair Market started in the culinary shop of Charlottesville's The Happy Cook. When she began working with Leslie Gregg at Gregg & Co, she met Hillary Horn. Soon, they started a catering business together. Hillary presented a business plan to Tiger Fuel when the old Gulf Station was chosen as a potential site for fast and fresh food in Cville.

Tiger Fuel knew that, demographically, they would need a unique look for their deli/gas station, and store combination. So, they hired local architect Bethany Puppolo, who used comfortable, local architectural features for the design. Since then, Bellair Market has weathered the test of time. Pat came on as co-manager with Hilary Horn and is still there, enjoying the energy and quality of what they produce every day.

Bellair Market has been highlighted in *Gourmet* magazine, *Virginia Living, The Washington Post,* and various other publications. They are generously sharing one of Melissa's favorite sandwich recipes.

Bellair Market's
Jefferson Sandwich

Boar's Head maple turkey
White cheddar cheese
Lettuce
Herb mayo (mayonnaise, whole-grain mustard, vinegar, dill)
Cranberry relish (Bellair purchases this product and grinds it to make a sauce. It has whole cranberries, cinnamon stick, and brandied pecans. Outrageous!)
French bread

Lay 4 slices of bread on a cutting board and spread with herb mayo. Top with the lettuce, cheese, and cranberry relish. Add a layer of maple turkey. Spread remaining herb mayo on the remaining 4 slices of bread and place spread-side down on top of sandwiches.

Cut each sandwich in half to serve.

Uncle Frank's
Hearty Heart-Healthy Chili

2 tablespoons canola oil
1½ cups chopped yellow onion
1 cup chopped red bell pepper
2 tablespoons minced garlic
2–3 serrano peppers, stemmed, seeded, and
    minced
1 medium zucchini, diced
2 cups fresh corn kernels (about 3 ears)
1½ pounds portobello mushrooms (about 5 large),
    stemmed, wiped clean, and cubed
2 tablespoons chili powder
1 tablespoon ground cumin
1¼ teaspoons kosher salt
¼ teaspoon cayenne pepper
4 large tomatoes, peeled, seeded, and chopped
2 cups canned black beans, plus 2 cups canned
    kidney beans, drained and rinsed
1 can (15 ounces) tomato sauce
1 cup vegetable stock
¼ cup chopped fresh cilantro
Cooked brown rice
Fat-free sour cream or strained plain yogurt
Diced avocado (optional)
Chopped scallions (green onions; optional)

In a large heavy pot, heat oil over medium-high heat. Add the onions, bell pepper, garlic, and serrano peppers. Cook, stirring until soft, about 3 minutes. Add the zucchini, corn, and mushrooms, and continue to cook and stir until they soften and vegetables start to brown around the edges, about 6 minutes. Add chili powder, cumin, salt, and cayenne, and cook (still stirring!), about 30 seconds. Add tomatoes, beans, tomato sauce, and vegetable stock. Stir well, and bring to a boil. Reduce the heat to medium-low and simmer, stirring occasionally, about 20 minutes.

Remove from the heat, and stir in the cilantro. Adjust seasoning to taste. Fill your bowl with ¼ cup of brown rice and ladle the chili on top. Be generous—it's heart healthy!

Top each serving with a dollop of fat-free sour cream or yogurt, and if you like, some spoonfuls of avocado and scallions. Enjoy!

Uncle Frank's
Jambalaya

Dry Spice Mix
1 large bay leaf, crumbled
½ tablespoon crushed red pepper flakes
1 tablespoon basil
1 teaspoon thyme
1 teaspoon paprika
1 teaspoon kosher salt
1 teaspoon cayenne pepper
½ teaspoon ground black pepper
½ teaspoon ground white pepper
1½ sticks butter
1 cup celery, roughly chopped
1 cup green and red bell pepper, roughly chopped
1¼ cups yellow onion, roughly chopped
2 jalapeño peppers—stems, membrane, and seeds
　　removed—diced
Peanut oil
1 pound boneless chicken thighs, roughly chopped
½ cup marsala wine, divided
2 pounds andouille sausage, roughly chopped, or
　　1 pound andouille and 1 pound chopped ham
　　(preferably Bashir's)
½ pound tasso, roughly chopped
1 cup chicken stock or broth
2 cans (28 ounces) crushed tomatoes
1 pound crawfish tails or shrimp
4–5 cups cooked rice

In a small bowl, combine all the ingredients for the spice mixture. Mix well and set aside.

In a large pot, melt the butter over high heat. Add the celery, bell peppers, and onions. Stir well, and cook until onions are translucent.

While they cook, heat peanut oil in a large skillet on high heat. Brown the chicken thighs, letting them get crusty on one side before turning over and browning the other side. Remove the chicken to a bowl. Add ¼ cup of the marsala wine and deglaze the pan, scraping up all the good bits. Add this cooking gold to the chicken and set pan aside.

Lower heat to medium on pan containing the veggies. Add the jalapeño peppers, sausage, ham (if using), tasso, cooked chicken, and the spice mix. Stir well and cook, about 10 minutes. Add the other ¼ cup of wine. Scrape the bottom of the pan to prevent scorching. Cook additional 5 minutes. Add the stock, and cook another 5 minutes, stirring occasionally. When the mixture begins to bubble, add the crushed tomatoes and stir well.

Reduce the heat to low, and simmer the jambalaya for 30 minutes, stirring occasionally. Add the peeled and deveined shrimp, and let them cook in the hot mixture for 5 minutes. Ten minutes before serving, add the rice and mix well. Let this cook on low. Serve in bowls.

Desserts & Cocktails

While Virginia has a very distinct apple season in the fall, peaches dominate the summertime. **Chiles Peach Orchard** has perfected the peach-picking experience. After an almost freeze-out in 1974, when there was not enough fruit to hire seasonal pickers, they allowed the public to come in and pick their own peaches. It has been an option at the Chiles Family Orchards ever since and part of the visiting experience.

Besides the beautiful property, other draws are the local products they sell and their peach frozen yogurt. On a hot Virginia summer day, the peach frozen yogurt is so refreshing. Unfortunately, they don't package it, so you can only eat it there.

This is a peach frozen yogurt recipe to have at home. While it is not the same as the one served at Chiles, it's a great opportunity to use some of the peaches picked there.

Fresh Peach Frozen Yogurt

(yields about 1 quart)

4 large, ripe peaches, cut into chunks
    (about 3 cups)
½ cup sugar
Juice of ½ lemon
2 cups plain, whole-milk yogurt

Combine the peaches, sugar, and lemon juice in a bowl. Cover bowl with piece of plastic wrap, and let sit for 2 hours. Stir every 20 minutes or so to let the peaches macerate.

Transfer peaches to a food processor or blender and purée. Put peach mixture in a large bowl, and stir in the yogurt. Chill in the refrigerator for at least an hour.

Freeze in an ice cream maker according to the directions. Serve immediately, or transfer to a container and allow to firm up for 1–2 hours in the freezer—it makes for better scooping. Serve with a slice of fresh peach and a sprig of mint.

BODO'S Bagels

You can't talk about food in Charlottesville without talking about BODO'S Bagels. As someone who used to live eight blocks from the once-famous H&H bagels in Manhattan, the fact that I am perhaps detrimentally addicted to BODO'S Bagels in Charlottesville is a testimony to their craft.

BODO'S
Bread Pudding

Cherry and Chocolate BODO'S Bagel Bread Pudding

3 large eggs
1 large egg yolk
1 cup sugar
1 tablespoon pure vanilla extract
¼ teaspoon ground cinnamon
1 teaspoon orange zest
2 cups whipping cream
1 cup whole milk
4 or 5 BODO'S plain bagels, cut into ½-inch cubes (8 cups)
1 cup chocolate chips
¾ cup dried cherries
Vanilla ice cream for serving

Whisk together eggs, egg yolk, sugar, vanilla, cinnamon, and orange zest in a large bowl until smooth. Whisk in heavy cream and milk. Add bagel cubes, and toss to coat. Let mixture sit, stirring occasionally, until bread absorbs some of the liquid, about 1 hour.

Preheat oven to 325°F. Grease an 8-inch square baking dish (2 inches deep). Stir chocolate chips and dried cherries into bagel mixture and transfer to dish. Bake until top is golden brown, and a toothpick inserted in center comes out clean, about 1 hour. If top browns too quickly, tent with foil. Let cool completely. Cut into squares, and serve with ice cream.

Vanilla Panna Cotta

Vanilla Panna Cotta with Grapefruit Tequila Gelatin

This recipe was adapted from the blog of Kayley of The Kitchen McCabe. She develops her own recipes that always feature an amazing combination of flavors.

Coconut Vanilla Panna Cotta
1 can (14 ounces) coconut milk
3 tablespoons sugar
½ vanilla bean, slit and seeds scraped
2 tablespoons water
1½ teaspoons gelatin (powdered)

Pour 2 tablespoons of water into a small bowl. Sprinkle gelatin over water. Allow 5 minutes to bloom.

Place coconut milk, sugar, and vanilla bean in a small saucepan. Bring just to a simmer. Remove from the heat, and add bloomed gelatin to the pan. Whisk the coconut milk/gelatin mixture until the gelatin has completely dissolved. Discard the vanilla bean, scraping out any remaining vanilla beans and adding them back into the coconut mixture.

Divide the panna cotta mixture evenly between 4 ramekins. Refrigerate for at least 3 hours, or until firmly set.

Grapefruit Tequila Gelatin
½ cup fresh grapefruit juice, divided
1 shot of tequila (any kind)
¾ teaspoon powdered gelatin
1 tablespoon sugar
1 grapefruit, segmented
Mint leaves, for garnish

Divide the panna cotta mixture evenly between four ½-cup dishes or ramekins. Refrigerate the panna cotta for at least 3 hours, or until firmly set.

To make the grapefruit gelatin, place 2 tablespoons of grapefruit juice in a small bowl. Sprinkle the gelatin over the juice, and allow it to bloom for 5 minutes.

Place the remaining grapefruit juice and 1 tablespoon of sugar in a small saucepan. Bring the juice to a boil, and add the bloomed gelatin. Whisk the gelatin into the grapefruit juice until it has fully dissolved. Remove from heat. Add 1 shot of tequila, mix well.

Remove the chilled panna cottas from the fridge, and place 2–3 segmented grapefruit slices on top of each one. Pour the grapefruit gelatin into each of the panna cotta glasses so that it almost covers the grapefruit slices.

Refrigerate for another hour, or until the gelatin has set.

Chef Alex Sorenson Col '00

Chef Alex Sorenson's culinary career started with a part-time prep cook job at the Buddhist Biker Bar & Grill while getting his undergraduate degree in cognitive science and computer science at UVA. He pursued a career in software development, but his passion for cooking, sparked by his mother's excellent home cooking and a childhood spent traipsing around Europe, finally got the better of him. In 2004, he ditched software, took a kitchen internship, and hasn't looked back.

Alex has cooked in some of New York City's top kitchens, producing everything from intimate dinners for heads of state to multicourse gala dinners for nearly 1,000 guests. Alex draws inspiration from his explorations of the rich culinary traditions found around the world. He has had the fortune to learn to cook frogs and all their parts with taxi drivers in Phnom Penh, Cambodia, make handmade pastas in ancient Tuscan farmhouses, forage and cook myriad wild ingredients in the jungles of Laos, brew traditional rice wine in Borneo, butcher and cook wildebeest and springbok in South Africa, and make pâté in France.

To become better acquainted with his ingredients, he took a break from the kitchen to work on small organic farms in France. He learned valuable lessons raising pigs in Normandy, picking grapes in Bordeaux, herding goats and cows, making cheese, plucking chickens, foraging for wild mushrooms, and cooking in farmhouse kitchens. These experiences further solidified his dedication to the support of sustainable, local farming and a cooking style highlighting, with restraint and sophistication, the natural bounty of a region.

In 2011, Alex was the opening chef for Colonie, a New American restaurant in Brooklyn, for which he earned a *New York Times* star. His cooking was described as "not overexposed or needlessly trendy...there is a brightness to it, a clever happiness that comes through on the plate. [He] does well by the forest floor and is a wizard with mushrooms."

In 2012, Alex left New York City to take the helm at Heaven Restaurant in Rwanda. Founded as a social enterprise, the restaurant has a mission of providing training, employment, and job skills. The deeper purpose was something Alex had found missing in much of his career, and he embraced the challenge of teaching and helping develop the quality of hospitality in a country needing increased tourism. The restaurant was consistently ranked as the top fine-dining destination in Rwanda.

Alex then spent a year in Malaysian Borneo, consulting on culinary projects and revisiting his software background to develop the FoodTranslator app. Unable to find a good tool to delve into local foods when traveling, he built it himself. It provides translations of food vocabulary and local dish descriptions in six languages and growing.

Now based in Brooklyn, Alex founded Blank Slate Kitchen, a company crafting ingredients to enable people to explore, develop, and realize their own kitchen creativity. Its first products, Rich Simple Syrups, are suitable for use in fine cocktails, desserts, and more. The ingredients and flavors are inspired by his explorations of foods worldwide—from Ugandan vanilla plantations to Zanzibar spice markets to Cambodian pepper farms to his own backyard garden in Borneo.

The Sticky Date Cake and Salted Crème Fraiche Ice Cream were on Alex's first draft of the opening menu for Colonie and have remained a customer favorite. The rich, sweet decadence of the date cake and toffee sauce are balanced and cut by the acidic tang and the salt of the ice cream.

Sticky Date Cake

16 ounces dates, pitted and stems removed
2 teaspoons vanilla extract
2 teaspoons baking soda
4 ounces unsalted butter, softened
2 cups sugar
2 large eggs
1¾ cups flour
2 teaspoons baking powder
1 teaspoon salt

Bring dates to a boil, and simmer for 5 minutes in enough water to cover them by a half inch. Strain (save the water), and puree the dates with 1 cup of the cooking water and the vanilla extract until completely smooth. Blend in baking soda.

Cream butter and sugar, then beat in eggs, baking powder, and salt. Add ⅓ of the flour, then ⅓ of the date puree, mixing until combined. Continue adding ⅓ of each until fully combined, but do not over mix.

Preheat oven to 350°F. Butter an 8x12 (or similar size) baking pan. Fill halfway with the batter. While the cake is baking, make the toffee sauce (below). Bake cake for 20 minutes, and remove from oven. The edges should be setting, but the center will still be loose. Poke holes with a thin skewer or fork all over the cake. Drizzle about ¼ cup of the warm toffee sauce over it. Return to oven, and bake for 10 minutes more, or until set (a skewer inserted into the center should come out clean).

Serve warm with more of the warm toffee sauce drizzled over the top and a scoop of salted crème fraiche ice cream.

Toffee Sauce
4 tablespoons butter
1 cup heavy cream
12 ounces dark brown sugar
½ teaspoon salt
3 teaspoons dark rum

Bring all ingredients together to a simmer over medium heat, stirring frequently.

Ice Cream

Salted Crème Fraiche Ice Cream

3 cups heavy cream
2 cups milk
5 teaspoons salt
1 cup sugar, divided
6 large egg yolks
3 cups crème fraiche (substitute sour cream if you
    can't get crème fraiche)

Bring heavy cream, milk, salt, and ½ cup of sugar to a simmer. Whisk together egg yolks and remaining ½ cup of sugar in a large bowl. Gradually whisk hot cream into egg yolks and then return the mixture to the pot. Whisk over heat until it thickens to coat the back of a spoon.

Strain through a fine mesh strainer. Mix in crème fraiche and chill. Process according to your ice cream maker's instructions.

The following rye-based cocktail with tart cherry juice is the perfect way to celebrate those most delicious of summer berries. The tart cherry juice, sour lime juice, caramel sweetness, and tangy spice of the Black Pepper Rich Simple Syrup all pair beautifully with the spicy kick of rye whiskey to create a sublime summer afternoon tipple.

Black and Red

½ ounce Blank Slate Kitchen Black Pepper Rich Simple Syrup
2 ounces rye whiskey
2 ounces tart cherry juice
½ ounce lime juice

Shake all ingredients together and strain into a rocks glass with ice.

Diane Boyer NURS '80

After completing a B.S. in biology, Diane Boyer moved to Charlottesville, Virginia, to enroll in the UVA School of Nursing. While in school for the second time, she became a vegetarian to save money and joined a computer science dining group. Each week, one person would prepare a meal for the group. As time passed, it became an enjoyable competition for the weekly chef to try to outdo the vegetarian meal from the previous week. Diane learned a great deal about creating delicious vegetarian meals and the significance of using fresh local food.

After graduating from UVA in 1980 as a registered nurse, Diane worked in the newborn intensive care unit (NICU) at the University of Virginia Medical Center. To escape the overwhelming world of work in a NICU, she came to love the countryside of Charlottesville and Albemarle County, becoming familiar with the native vegetation through long bike rides. She picked strawberries and blackberries, and her bike adventures helped Diane locate abundant sources of blackberries.

Diane's love of bike riding and personal conflict with treatment methods in the early years of neonatalogy eventually led her to explore India, Nepal, and France by bike. After returning to Charlottesville, Diane went to graduate school and obtained a Master's in psychiatric nursing.

During this time, Diane met her husband in the Health Science Library. They shared a love of contra dancing, clogging, and eating good food. She lived on a farm very close to Charlottesville, on the side of Carter's Mountain, that was rich in wineberry bushes. Going back to her creative cooking roots, Diane wondered what to do with these fresh berries. Researching berry pie and experimenting with different piecrust recipes, Diane aimed to make the ultimate flakey, buttery, and slightly sweet piecrust. In fact, her friends and family now comment on the perfection of her piecrust. Over time, Diane moved from strawberry and blackberry pie to a combination of berries. When a fresh source of local raspberries became available, Diane was able to experiment with raspberries instead of wineberries in the pie mixture.

After marriage and a son, who eventually became old enough to help with berry picking and making piecrust dough, requests for the warm, juicy, flakey multiberry pie increased. Diane has wonderful summer memories of mass-producing them with her son and enjoying them with family and friends.

Multiberry Pie

Pie Crust
2½ cups unbleached, all-purpose flour
2 tablespoons granulated sugar
1 teaspoon salt
8 tablespoons salted butter, chilled
6 tablespoons Crisco, chilled
4–5 tablespoons ice water, as needed

Filling
4 cups blackberries
1 cup wineberries or raspberries
1 cup strawberries, sliced
1 cup sugar
1 teaspoon cinnamon
½ teaspoon ground ginger
Dash of nutmeg
3 tablespoons lemon juice
3 tablespoons quick-cooking tapioca
3 tablespoons butter

Begin by making the piecrust. Sift together flour, sugar, and salt into a mixing bowl. Add chilled butter and Crisco. Working quickly and using your fingertips, rub butter and Crisco into dry ingredients until the mixture resembles coarse meal. Add ice water one tablespoon at a time, tossing flour mixture with a fork.

Turn dough, and knead until it forms a ball. Wrap in waxed paper. Chill at least 2 hours in the refrigerator.

Preheat oven to 425°F. Lightly flour your work surface. Cover the top of the dough with waxed paper or a pastry cloth. Roll out ¾ of dough to ¼-inch thickness on a floured surface, forming a circle. Line a 9-inch pie plate with the dough. Insert foil filled with beans or rice, and prebake for 8 minutes. Then remove foil, and prick the bottom of dough with a fork. Return to oven for another 10–13 minutes, or until piecrust is golden brown. Remove from oven and allow to cool.

Wash and stem the berries. Place berries in a wide pot over medium heat. Add the sugar, spices, tapioca, and lemon juice. Cook until just boiling. Remove from heat and add to piecrust.

Preheat oven to 350°F. Roll out the remaining piecrust dough and cover the pie. Crimp the edges, and cut 4–5 vents around the top of the pie. Bake for 30 minutes, or until top crust is golden brown and filling is bubbling.

Let the pie cool for at least 1 hour before serving. It is delicious alone or with vanilla ice cream. It can be gently reheated.

Sandy Caldwell COL '80
& Meg Swab CURRY '12

BUSINESS ANALYST, UVA ATHLETICS

When 18-year-old Sandy McFadden first stepped on Grounds back in August 1976, she knew that she had come to a very special place. Her four years at UVA opened her eyes to a vast, engaging, fascinating world beyond her home in Tidewater, Virginia. From her first "Guys in Ties, Girls in Pearls" football game to walking the ceremonious lawn just a few years later, her time in Charlottesville made an everlasting impact. Sandy fondly recalls evenings out at the Mousetrap, studying on the Lawn with her sisters from Delta Zeta, and her first classic Grillswith donut and ice cream sandwich served by Ethel. Though the Mousetrap has long since been replaced by other eateries (presently occupied by the delicious burger joint Boylan Heights), the allure of Charlottesville's unique culture still calls her back to the Blue Ridge.

After Sandy married Doug Caldwell (Dartmouth '76) in October 1983, the couple settled in Alexandria, Virginia, to start their family. Its close proximity to Charlottesville enabled them to take trips to 'Hooville over the years, especially to cheer on the Cavaliers at Scott Stadium.

Nearly three decades after Sandy's time at UVA, it was time for her daughter, Meg, to decide which university to attend. During the intervening time, Charlottesville had continually changed, adapted, and expanded. Yet one thing remained—the pull that Meg felt toward the orange and blue was the exact same one her mom had felt many years before.

Following in her mom's footsteps, Meg enjoyed the various restaurants on the Corner and became a sister in Delta Zeta. She then stretched a bit further and forged her own path, working in the Athletics Department. Some of Meg's fondest memories include working in academic affairs, tutoring student-athletes in Spanish, and working in Football Operations. These opportunities allowed her to work in professional sports for a few years before return-

ing to Charlottesville in November 2013 to work in the Athletics Business Office.

It is safe to say that in these two generations of Caldwell women, orange and blue run in their veins. To that end, the Chocolate Chip Sour Cream Cake, from Sandy Dooley, Sandy's college roommate, is a versatile dish that makes for an ideal brunch item for those early afternoon tailgates by Scott Stadium.

Sandy and Meg's affinity for the magical town known as Charlottesville grows stronger each passing year. No matter where they may live or travel, it will always feel like home.

Chocolate Chip Sour Cream Cake

½ cup butter
1½ cups sugar, divided
2 large eggs
2 cups flour
1 teaspoon baking soda
1 cup sour cream
2 tablespoons milk
1½ teaspoons vanilla
12 ounces semisweet chocolate chips
2 teaspoons cinnamon
Confectioners sugar

Preheat oven to 350°F. If using a dark, nonstick pan, you may want to reduce oven temp to 325°F.

Using an electric mixer, cream together butter and 1 cup of sugar. Beat in eggs, one at a time, until mixture is light and fluffy.

In a separate bowl, combine the flour and baking soda.

In another bowl, combine the sour cream and milk.

Alternate adding the flour and baking soda mix and the milk and sour cream mix to the butter, sugar, and egg mix. This works best if you start and end with the dry ingredients. Add vanilla and then gently fold in chocolate chips.

Pour half the batter into a greased and floured Bundt pan. Sprinkle cinnamon and the remaining ½ cup of sugar on top of the first layer. Spread the remaining half of the batter on top of the cinnamon sugar.

Bake for 50 minutes, or until golden brown. Allow cake pan to cool on a wire rack for 15 minutes. Run a knife along the sides of the Bundt pan to loosen the cake. Flip the Bundt pan over onto a plate. Dust with confectioners sugar and enjoy!

Sarah Lanzman's

Persimmon Mousse

Persimmon Mousse with Pomegranate Molasses and Fresh Pomegranate Seeds

(serves 6)

4 large, ripe, soft Hachiya persimmons
2 teaspoons baking soda
1 cup cold water
3 tablespoons unflavored gelatin or agar-agar
    (vegetarian gelatin)
2 cups apple juice
2 cups frozen yogurt
Pomegranate molasses (available at Grand Market
    or Foods of All Nations)
Fresh mint sprigs for garnish
Seeds from 1 ripe pomegranate

Halve the persimmons, pick out any seeds, and scrape the soft pulp from the skin. Purée and then measure out 2 cups.

Note: Do not leave the persimmons out too long. They must be used right away or they will brown.

Dissolve the gelatin in 1 cup of water in a small bowl. Bring the apple juice to a boil, stir in the dissolved gelatin, and continue to cook, while stirring, for 5 minutes. Add the persimmon puree, stir thoroughly and then remove from the heat. Let cool for 1 minute. Stir in the baking soda until incorporated.

Pour into a glass bowl, and cover with plastic wrap directly on the surface of the jelly. Chill for at least 2 hours to set, but overnight is better.

After It has set, blend with the frozen yogurt in a blender or food processor until it is whipped. Scoop it into glasses. Drizzle pomegranate molasses over the mousse. Garnish with fresh pomegranate seeds and a mint sprig.

Amy Clobes, Ph.D. ENGR '14

DIRECTOR OF PROFESSIONAL DEVELOPMENT, OFFICE OF GRADUATE AND POSTDOCTORAL AFFAIRS

Amy Clobes joined the Office of Graduate and Postdoctoral Affairs after earning her Ph.D. from UVA in 2014. As Director of Professional Development, she collaborates with faculty and partners across Grounds to provide career and professional development training, advising, and resources to graduate students and postdoctoral trainees at UVA.

Amy enjoys meeting new people and learning about their unique experiences and passions. In particular, she loves the way food brings people together to create these conversations. While working on her doctorate, Amy used baking to satisfy her sweet tooth, explore new recipes, and build community with her fellow students and faculty by sharing her sweet treats.

People often ask Amy what her favorite thing is to bake, or whether she has a signature recipe. Her specialty is in variety—cakes, cookies, pies, bars, and more. Whether it's an old family recipe she has recently rediscovered or a new trend in indulgent desserts, Amy has a passion for learning and mastering new recipes and techniques. She is always excited to give something a try!

She does have a penchant for all things chocolate, and this chocolate cupcake recipe has the right combination of being both simple and decadent. These are ultra-rich but fairly simple because they aren't completely from scratch. (Shh, don't tell your guests how easy these were to make!)

Chocolate Cupcakes
Decadent Chocolate Cupcakes with Chocolate Frosting

(yields 24 cupcakes)

1 box (15.25 ounces) of chocolate cake mix
1 box (3.4 ounces) of instant pudding mix
¾ cup sour cream
¾ cup canola oil
4 large eggs
½ cup warm water

Frosting
4 sticks (2 cups) unsalted butter, room temperature
1 pound confectioners sugar
2 teaspoons pure vanilla extract
2 tablespoons heavy cream or milk
1 cup semisweet chocolate chips, melted and cooled
½ cup unsweetened cocoa powder

Preheat oven to 350°F. Line muffin tin with paper liners or spray with nonstick cooking spray.

Using a mixer, slowly beat together the cake and pudding mixes (I prefer Duncan Hines Devil's Food), sour cream, oil, eggs, vanilla, and water. Once ingredients are wet, increase to medium speed and mix about 2 minutes, or until well combined.

Scoop batter into 24 muffin wells, with a scant 3 tablespoons per well. Bake for 16 minutes, or until a toothpick comes out clean. Cool in muffin tin for about 10 minutes and then remove cupcakes from muffin tin and finish cooling on a wire rack.

While the cupcakes are cooling, make the frosting. Using a mixer, beat the butter on medium-high speed for about 5 minutes. Turn the mixer to low speed, and gradually add in the confectioners sugar until it is completely incorporated. Add in vanilla and heavy cream or milk. Turn mixer speed back to medium-high and beat for 3–4 minutes, until light and fluffy. Add in the cooled, melted chocolate and beat until well incorporated. Add in cocoa powder slowly, beating on low speed after each addition to avoid sending the cocoa powder everywhere. Then increase to medium-high to fully incorporate.

Frost cupcakes as desired.

Becky Davis

EXECUTIVE ASSISTANT TO THE ATHLETICS DIRECTOR

Becky Davis' career at UVA started in March 1980 in the Purchasing Department on the top floor of Madison Hall. Those were the days of IBM Selectric typewriters. There was no World Wide Web or e-mail.

In November 1985, she transferred to the Athletics Department to work for the athletics director, Dick Schultz, and has worked for each athletics director since. During her time in the Athletics Department, Becky has seen several new facilities built, three varsity sports added, and watched the program enjoy much success. Becky is grateful for the many experiences she has been blessed with while working at the University of Virginia and for the lifelong friendships that have developed.

Becky has used this recipe for many years. It came from the back of a Libby's Pure Pumpkin can. Pumpkin rolls are a favorite of Becky's family and friends, and she has given away many as gifts. Her Aunt Dorothy made the first pumpkin roll she ever tasted when she sent slices with Becky and her cousin on their trip to the 1987 All-American Bowl, where UVA beat BYU 22–16.

Pumpkin Roll

¼ cup powdered sugar to sprinkle on towel
¾ cup all-purpose flour
½ teaspoon baking powder
½ teaspoon baking soda
½ teaspoon ground cinnamon
½ teaspoon ground cloves
¼ teaspoon salt
3 large eggs
1 cup granulated sugar
⅔ cup pumpkin

Filling
1 package (8 ounces) of cream cheese, at room
     temperature
1 cup powdered sugar, sifted
6 tablespoons butter or margarine, softened
1 teaspoon vanilla extract

Preheat oven to 375°F. Grease 15x10 jelly roll pan and line with waxed paper. Grease and flour paper. Sprinkle a thin, cotton kitchen towel with powdered sugar.

Combine flour, baking powder, baking soda, cinnamon, cloves, and salt in small bowl. Beat eggs and granulated sugar in large mixer bowl until thick. Beat in pumpkin. Stir in flour mixture. Spread evenly into prepared pan.

Bake for 13–15 minutes, or until top of cake springs back when touched. (If using a dark-colored pan, begin checking for doneness at 11 minutes.) Immediately loosen and turn cake onto prepared towel. Carefully peel off paper. Roll up cake and towel together, starting with narrow end. Cool on wire rack.

While the cake cools, prepare the filling. Beat the cream cheese, powdered sugar, butter, and vanilla extract in small mixer bowl until smooth.

Carefully unroll the cake. Spread the cream cheese mixture over cake and then reroll. Wrap in plastic wrap or aluminum foil, and refrigerate at least an hour. Sprinkle with powdered sugar before serving, if desired.

Note: Be sure to put enough powdered sugar on the towel when rolling up the cake so it will not stick. The secret to the cake not splitting when unrolling is to make sure it cools completely. If the cake splits, prepare another batch of filling and frost the outside of the pumpkin roll. It's doubly delicious, and no one is the wiser.

The Libby's recipe also calls for 1 cup of walnuts in the cake, if desired. Trim up the ends for a nice presentation.

Chelsea Shine Wilson & Tyler Wilson Col '12, Col '11

SPORTS BROADCASTING ANALYST, PROFESSIONAL BASEBALL PLAYER

Chelsea Shine and Tyler Wilson met at UVA during their time as student-athletes. Chelsea was a basketball player, while Tyler played baseball. As athletes, it was important to pay attention to food and nutrition, but growing up with a mom who loved to bake meant Chelsea had a strong sweet tooth.

Although Tyler didn't grow up with much of a sweet tooth, he certainly has one now, thanks to Chelsea's frequent baking. Chelsea's mom was known around the neighborhood for her delicious chocolate chip cookies. Friends always asked for "Mrs. Shine's cookies" when they were around. When Chelsea left home for UVA, she set out to perfect this recipe since she would be missing her daily supply.

Chelsea is a broadcast sports analyst, primarily covering women's college basketball. She does freelance work and has covered women's college hoops with Raycom Sports Network, ESPN3, and Fox Sports since 2013. She also serves as an analyst for WINA 1070, a local Charlottesville radio station, and the ACC Network Extra, covering the UVA women's basketball team. She previously worked for the Virginia Athletics Foundation in a variety of roles. Her love of women's basketball and UVA is a big part of why she still loves Cville and maintains so many relationships there.

After graduation, Tyler continued his dream of playing baseball. He has been a pitcher in the Baltimore Orioles organization since he was drafted by them in 2011. He made his major league debut in May 2015 and has served as both a starting pitcher and a reliever. His brother, Riley Wilson, is currently a third year and a pitcher on the UVA baseball team.

Chelsea and Tyler love getting to still be involved in Virginia athletics. They met some of their best friends through the tight-knit student-athlete community, and baking cookies was a sure way to get a big crowd over during the week! The University and Charlottesville communities gave them so much during their time on Grounds and now as alumni. They will always call Cville home, and orange and blue will forever be their favorite colors.

Chocolate Chip Cookies

2¼ cups all-purpose flour
1 teaspoon baking soda
1 teaspoon salt
1 cup (2 sticks) butter, softened
¾ cup granulated sugar
1 cup packed brown sugar
1 teaspoon vanilla extract
2 large eggs
1 package (12 ounces) Nestlé® Toll House®
    Semi-Sweet Chocolate Morsels

Preheat oven to 375°F. Combine flour, baking soda, and salt in small bowl. Beat butter, granulated sugar, brown sugar, and vanilla extract in large mixer bowl until creamy. Add eggs, one at a time, beating well after each addition. Gradually beat in flour mixture.

Stir in morsels. Drop by rounded tablespoon onto ungreased baking sheets.

Bake for 9–11 minutes, or until golden brown. Cool on baking sheets for 2 minutes. Remove to wire racks to cool completely.

Lauren Adler Col '89

FOUNDER OF CHOCOLOPOLIS

Popping a square of Bonnat's Madagascar chocolate into her mouth, Lauren Adler was surprised to find bursts of red fruit and citrus taking over her senses. Despite her lifelong love of chocolate, she discovered she had never tasted the best chocolate has to offer and, more importantly, that dark chocolate doesn't have to taste bitter. Lauren had found her calling.

Opening a chocolate store wasn't always her plan, though. Lauren originally arrived at UVA with dreams of working on Wall Street. Much to her dormmates' amusement, she attended recruiting sessions during her first year to see what investment banks looked for in new employees. Deciding they were interested in intelligent people with critical-thinking and problem-solving skills, Lauren decided to major in history.

After four years on Wall Street, Lauren went on to earn her MBA from Dartmouth and began working at a supermarket chain in Boston, where her love of the food-retailing business was cemented. Suddenly, she couldn't stop thinking about her own ideas for retail stores, but the timing wasn't right yet.

Instead, Lauren went on to spend almost fours year at Amazon during its early days, but she couldn't shake the dream of opening a specialty food retail business. After marrying her husband Mark, a Darden graduate, there was no delaying anymore.

Since its opening in Seattle, Washington, in 2008, Chocolopolis has become one of the most renowned specialty chocolate stores in the country, and Lauren has become an expert on the craft chocolate market. Four of Chocolopolis' handcrafted truffles have won medals at the International Chocolate Awards, with three of them advancing to win medals at the World Final in London. The store offers a full menu of drinking chocolate from many cacao-growing regions, as well as chocolate drinks infused with herbs and spices. The chocolate recommended in this recipe can be purchased from Chocolopolis.

Thomas Jefferson and his family regularly drank chocolate, and this recipe was created using ingredients commonly available during his era. To keep with historical accuracy, this recipe was designed using water, but you can substitute an equal amount of milk, rice milk, or other liquid if you prefer. Just be sure to keep the heat on a very low setting and stir constantly. Lauren also recommends splurging on high-quality, single-origin chocolate with minimal ingredients. The flavor of your drinking chocolate is entirely dependent on the quality of the chocolate you use.

"The superiority of chocolate both for health and nourishment will soon give it the same preference over tea & coffee in America which it has in Spain where they can get it by a single voiage, & of course while it is sweet."

Letter from Thomas Jefferson to John Adams,
November 27, 1785.

Mr. Jefferson's Drinking Chocolate

(serves 2)

1½ cup water
2 ounces, or ⅓ cup Venezuela-origin chocolate disks, preferably Felchlin Maracaibo 65 percent or Valrhona Araguani 72 percent
¼ teaspoon freshly ground nutmeg
½ teaspoon cinnamon
3 whole cloves
⅛ heaping teaspoon crushed red pepper

Bring the water to a slow simmer in a saucepan. Meanwhile, measure the chocolate and spices and set aside.

When the water reaches a simmer, turn the heat down to the lowest setting, and add the chocolate and spices. Stir continuously to prevent burning. Let the mixture steep on the lowest heat for 8–10 minutes, depending on the desired thickness of your drink.

There may be a few simmering bubbles, but there shouldn't be many. Strain the chocolate into mugs and enjoy.

Note: If you have a molinillo, pour the chocolate into a high-sided pot and froth with the molinillo before serving. This will build up foam in the drink and make it an even more authentic colonial experience.

Mitch Frank Col '96

EDITOR OF *WINE SPECTATOR*

"You're going to be a pauper. I love you, and I'll always support you, but you're going to be a pauper." That's what Mitch Frank's father said when his son called him from the basement of Newcomb Hall to say he had found his passion in life—journalism.

Granted, being a magazine editor isn't the most lucrative career. But in the twenty years since he graduated, Mitch has found more success than he could have imagined that day. As associate editor of *Wine Spectator* and news editor of its website, he's been able to pursue his passions for food, wine, travel, and storytelling every day.

Virginia didn't have a journalism program during Mitch's undergrad years, but as an Echols Scholar, he was encouraged to explore everything the University had to offer, studying history, sociology, psychology, communications, and literature. One advisor, a former magazine editor, told him to learn about anything he found interesting; sooner or later, he'd get the chance to write about it.

Mitch says he had a second major—*The Cavalier Daily*. As a writer and then editor, he spent endless hours helping pull the student newspaper together five days a week. His time as the paper's executive editor gave him the opportunity to manage a staff and budget while still just a student. He also found love. His future wife, Catherine Shnaider (class of '99), worked at the paper, too.

During college, wine was not Mitch's beverage of choice; convincing his friends to buy better-quality beer was tough enough. But after graduation, when he'd visit Catherine, the couple explored the region's emerging wine scene. Wine became more of a passion when he worked as a political reporter for *Time* magazine. (Covering two presidential elections will make many people look for a drink at day's end.) When Mitch began looking for new challenges after the 2004 election, Catherine pointed to an issue of *Wine Spectator* and said, "That's the magazine you're excited to read when a new issue arrives."

Today, Mitch's favorite job is writing long-form profiles of winemakers. In wine, there's a concept of terroir—a wine's flavor is shaped by the land it came from, the soil and microclimate. It's also shaped by the people who make it—their desires, their histories, even the food they eat. After all, wine is made for pairing with food.

Virginia's wine history begins with Thomas Jefferson's glorious failure to grow European grape varieties. But his enthusiasm certainly inspired many of today's Virginia winemakers. In just the past twenty years, they have made huge strides in uncovering what the Old Dominion's terroir is best suited for. Now the fifth-biggest wine producer in the country, Virginia is a state to watch when it comes to wine.

Mitch Frank's **Virginia Wine Recommendations**

Barboursville Vineyards, Octagon, Virginia

Virginia is the Old Dominion but a young wine region, so Barboursville, now forty years old, counts as a pioneer and veteran. The Zonin family, highly successful vintners in Italy's Veneto, established the winery in 1976, at the nineteenth century Virginia governor James Barbour's estate. His mansion, now just a shell, was designed by Mr. Jefferson, and the winery's top red blend is named for the octagonal room at the home's heart. Winemaker and general manager Luca Paschina has worked since the '90s to understand the terroir of 150 acres of vines and improve winemaking. He has made great strides, making this a standard-bearer for the state.

RdV Vineyards, Lost Mountain, Virginia

Rutger de Vink launched one of Virginia's most ambitious wine projects when he planted his first vines in Faquier County in 2006. A former marine and IT executive, de Vink has gone all in from the start, building a state-of-the-art winery and hiring Eric Boissenot, one of Bordeaux's top consulting ecologists. His Bordeaux blends are outstanding.

Keswick Vineyards, Viognier, Monticello

De Vink, Steve Case—there is something about Virginia wine country that seems to attract high-tech entrepreneurs looking for a different life. Al Schornberg left a high-tech career in Michigan for Albermarle County because he and his wife, Cindy, wanted their kids to grow up on a farm. But they also saw potential in a young wine region. Keswick's Viognier shows what Virginia can do with the variety when it is treated well in the vineyard and cellar.

Michael Shaps, Tannat, Monticello

Michael Shaps was managing a Boston restaurant in the 1980s when he fell in love with wine. He studied winemaking in Burgundy but chose to return to the East Coast, starting work at Jefferson Vineyards in 1995. He opened his own winery a few years later. He also consults for other American wineries and co-owns Maison Shaps in France. His Tannat is powerful, yet focused and balanced.

King Family, Meritage, Monticello

Ellen and David King moved from Houston to Crozet in 1996 because they wanted a farm. But soon they were hearing their land had vineyard potential, so they quickly became grape growers and then winemakers. Now their three sons (including fellow Wahoo James) all work at the winery. Their red blend is very good and a good value.

Linden Vineyards, Petit Manseng, Late Harvest Virginia

Arguably no one has done more to bring recognition to the potential of Virginia's horse country as a wine region than Jim Law. He founded Linden on an old farm in 1983 after working at various wineries and serving in the Peace Corps. He has shown a deft hand with both red and white wines, but this dessert wine routinely delivers.

Mark Kutney

UVA ARCHITECTURAL CONSERVATOR

Mark Kutney is an architectural conservator with UVA Facilities. Coming from the Office of the Architect and now a member of the Facilities Department, he works with architectural consultants to develop plans for historic buildings on Grounds. Mark considers himself an advocate for the historical architecture of UVA, working with architects and tradespeople to minimize the impact on buildings during renovations while making necessary updates.

With a degree in biochemistry, a graduate of the Smithsonian Institute Conservation Training program, and ten years at Colonial Williamsburg in furniture and architectural conservation, Mark is engaged not only with the Rotunda's and Pavilion's renovations but making these buildings relevant for students today, too. For exam-

ple, after the renovation, the Rotunda now has an open student lounge, additional and updated classrooms, and more locations for students to study.

As part of a Pavilion X update, carpenters found letters in the walls when they started an electrical project. It is part of Mark's responsibility to go through historical materials found and collected onsite when new work is to be done, a kind of aboveground archaeology.

One of the recent discoveries in Pavilion X was a folded piece of paper with J. L. Cabell's name on it and a fruit cake recipe. Mark and UVA Special Collections are sharing this document for the first time, and Dr. Elizabeth O'Connell, food historian, has been generous to re-create the recipe.

Dr. Elizabeth O'Connell, Ph.D.

FOOD HISTORIAN Col '79, Grad '88

Dr. Libby Haight O'Connell is a cultural historian and author of *The American Plate: A Culinary History in 100 Bites.* She worked at the History Channel for twenty years, where she was Chief Historian and Senior Vice President for Corporate Social Responsibility. She has received four Emmys for her work in television and education.

In 2014, President Obama appointed Dr. O'Connell to the U.S. World War I Centennial Commission. She also serves on the Board of Trustees for the Thomas Jefferson Foundation and on the Kitchen Cabinet at the Smithsonian. Dr. O'Connell received her M.A. and Ph.D. in American history from the University of Virginia in 1988.

An Excellent Fruitcake Recipe

In 2016, the architectural conservator of the Jefferson-designed pavilions on the Lawn found an enigmatic paper addressed to James L. Cabell and a number of letters hidden inside the walls of Pavilion X. This paper, torn in parts, contains a partial list of ingredients for a very large fruitcake, or possibly four fruitcakes baked in large loaf pans. The list includes 2 pounds flour, 2 pounds sugar, and 2 pounds butter, plus raisins, citron, currants, and orange zest, along with 24 eggs. Nutmeg and mace are also on the list.

The size of the cake produced by this original recipe may surprise us today, but "receipts" for enormous fruitcakes can be found in many cookbooks from the eighteenth and nineteenth centuries. Thomas Jefferson's cousin, Mary Randolph, first published her very popular cookbook *The Virginia Housewife* in 1824. Her fruitcake "receipt" was double (!) the size of Mr. Cabell's. Sarah Josepha Hale, the Martha Stewart of her day, wrote a recipe for "Rich Plum Cake" in her *The Good Housekeeper* in the 1840s that is very similar in proportions to the list found inside Pavilion X. These giant recipes made large cakes for weddings, funerals, holidays, and election day. By the Civil War era, however, authors of fruitcake recipes for private households did not assume you were feeding a huge crowd.

For those of you who don't like fruitcake with those weird green cherries and dry texture, fear not. Nineteenth century cooks knew what they were doing. Their fruitcakes resemble something akin to a rich carrot cake, only with no carrots and 1½ cups of booze.

What follows is my version of fruitcake inspired by Mr. Cabell's torn recipe and the fruitcake recipes of his contemporaries. It will make two 8×4 loaves. I recommend making one loaf for slicing and using the rest of the batter to make mini-muffins.

Don't be put off by the long list of ingredients. Remember, this is a recipe inspired by history. It doesn't require any fancy technique. You may have to order some of the spices online or visit the Spice Diva in Charlottesville, which stocks all the spices needed. The fresher the spices, the better. That old tin of cloves way back on your spice shelf is not good enough for this recipe if you want to enjoy the full flavors of the nineteenth century. I had to order citron online, but otherwise, my local gourmet store had all the ingredients on hand.

Baked-on fruit can be hard to clean off a pan. I highly recommend lining your loaf pan with greased parchment paper. It also makes it much easier to remove the cooled cake from the pan. If you don't have parchment paper, aluminum foil will do. Cooking spray will not go amiss with all that butter, and we won't tell anyone. It's sort of the belt-and-suspenders approach to greasing the pans.

-Dr. Elizabeth O'Connell

Courtesy, Special Collections, University of Virginia Library:
RG-35/3/1.161.

Rich and Spicy Fruit Cake

(yields two 8x4 loaves)

The Fruits

1 cup golden raisins, chopped
1 cup dried currants
½ cup candied orange rind, diced
½ cup candied citron, diced
1 cup crystalized ginger, diced
Grated zest of 1 large orange

1 cup bourbon (or your favorite rum). Orange juice or apple
    cider may be substituted but will not be historically
    accurate.
2 sticks (½ pound) high-quality butter (Reserve 2 tablespoons
    for greasing the pans. Do not substitute margarine or
    imitation butter.)
1 cup white sugar
1 cup apple cider

The Spices

1 tablespoon ground cinnamon
2 teaspoons ground cloves
2 teaspoons ground allspice
2 teaspoons ground mace
2 teaspoons ground nutmeg

The Dry Ingredients

1¾ cups all-purpose flour, sifted
1 teaspoon baking powder
1 teaspoon baking soda
1½ teaspoons salt
2 large eggs, beaten lightly
1 cup chopped pecans or walnuts, toasted if possible
½ cup brandy or bourbon for basting after the cake is baked.

Preheat oven to 325°F.

With the 2 tablespoons of butter that have been set aside, generously grease two 8x4 loaf pans. Line with parchment paper and grease again. You can also use 1 loaf pan and 1 muffin pan.

Put the fruits, rinds, ginger, and zest (the first six ingredients) in a large, nonreactive pot. Add 1 cup bourbon and stir to mix the fruits, etc. Over low heat, bring the bourbon and fruit to a simmer, and cook gently for 5 minutes. This will soften the dried fruits and open their flavors. Add the remaining butter in chunks, and let it melt, stirring occasionally. Reduce the heat as low as possible, or turn it off, rather than burn the fruit. Stir in the sugar and mix well. You don't beat this batter; hand mixing with a large spoon is the right approach here. Pour in the cider and mix.

Now, add all the spices and stir some more, mixing thoroughly. Turn off the heat. Your kitchen will smell like heaven. Remove the pot from the burner, and let the ingredients cool.

At this point, you can set aside the batter and refrigerate it for up to 4 days. You could also freeze this for up to a month, and thaw overnight in the fridge when you are ready to use. Bring the batter back to room temperature to proceed.

Using a medium mixing bowl, it's time to sift the 1¾ cup flour together with the 1 teaspoon of baking powder, 1 teaspoon baking soda, and 1 ½ teaspoon salt. Gradually pour the dry ingredients into the fruit and bourbon batter, and stir until the dry ingredients are fully incorporated.

Add the 2 beaten eggs and stir well. The addition of modern baking powder and soda make it possible to leave out 10 more eggs. Add the cup of pecans, mixing just until they are fully distributed. Again, do not use a beater.

Fill your loaf pans. Center the pans in your preheated oven. Bake for 60 minutes. Check for doneness by inserting a toothpick. If it comes out clean, the cakes are done. If you are baking muffins, they only need 25 minutes.

Remove the pans from the oven, and set on trivets or on a heat-proof surface. Let cool. This is important. The cakes will fall apart if you try to get them out of the pans while they are hot.

While they are cooling, baste the cakes and muffins with ½ cup bourbon or brandy. If you have a basting brush, this is the time to use it. Or just gently drizzle the brandy over the cakes, especially around the edges, using a spoon. Take your time.

Once the cakes are cool, remove them from the pans. Wrap well and tightly seal in aluminum foil. They will keep for a couple weeks as long as they are tightly sealed and stay cool. The liquor acts as a preservative, so you can add a little more bourbon or brandy with your basting brush in a few days if you so desire. In the nineteenth century, these cakes might be wrapped in butter-dipped cheesecloth, wrapped again in bourbon-saturated linen to preserve them, and then stored in tins a cool place. More bourbon or brandy would be occasionally brushed or gently spooned on top to keep the cakes moist and fresh until it was time to serve them. You can do this, too.

Included is the 1841 recipe for Rich Plum Cake (or fruitcake) by Sarah Josepha Hale, editor of *Godey's Lady's Book* and author of *The Good Housekeeper*. Hale was writing while Mr. Cabell was at UVA. Note that there are no plums! A plum cake or plum pudding was a dessert plump with fruit, nuts, and/or candied rind.

1841 Rich Plum Cake

Take 2 pounds and a half of well-dried and sifted flour, allow the same quantity of fresh butter washed with rose water, 2 pounds of finely pounded loaf sugar, 3 pounds of cleaned and dried currants, 1 pound of raisins stoned, 1 nutmeg grated, ½ pound of sweetmeats cut small, ¼ pound of blanched almonds pounded with a little rose water, and 20 eggs (the yolks and whites separately beaten). The butter must be beaten by hand until it becomes like cream; then add the sugar and by degrees, the eggs.

After these, add the rest of the ingredients, mixing in at last the currants with a teacupful of rose or orange water. This mixture must be beaten together rather more than half an hour, then put into a cake pan, which has been buttered and lined with buttered paper; fill it rather more than ¾ full. It should be baked in a moderate oven for 3 hours and then cooled gradually by first letting it stand some time at the mouth of the oven. If you fear the bottom of the cake may burn, put the pan on a plate with sawdust between.

Sarah Josepha Hale, *The Good Housekeeper* (1841 edition)

(Mineola, NY: Dover Publications, 1996 reprint), 100.

About Melissa

Melissa Palombi works in the University of Virginia's Athletics Department in marketing and promotions, as well as assisting in licensing. She enjoys helping coordinate the Athletic Department's many events and is pleased to collaborate with the University Communications Department on all things with the UVA brand. For Melissa, who has a B.F.A. from Carnegie Mellon University and an M.A. in art history, this book is an expression of her pursuit of the creative. Her first cookbook was for her parents' thirty-fourth wedding anniversary, a compilation of both sides of her family heritage and passion for food. There were thirty-five recipes, thirty-four for the years together and one for good luck, plus many family photos. That was an unpublished gift, so it is very exciting to take Hoos in the Kitchen *to the next level.*

While Melissa works for the University, no University funds were spent in the creation of this book. It is purely a personal passion project and an awesome way to get to know her new community in Charlottesville. This book only touches the surface of the many talented University of Virginia alumni and staff who create community and tell their stories through food here in Charlottesville and throughout the country. She hopes to keep discovering these connections.

Melissa lives in Charlottesville with her partner, Holly, and is grateful to have her mother close by to visit in Wintergreen, Virginia, on weekends. They spend time in the mountains and enjoy exploring the ever-evolving local food scene.

About Sarah

Col '05

Sarah Cramer Shields specializes in environmental portraiture. Her focus is documenting her subjects with honest, accurate portraits. Her passion for food and stories stems from a life filled with exposure to culture and travel. Dual degrees from the University of Virginia in fine art photography and anthropology serve as a natural extension of her passion for understanding people and making beautiful images.

"For as long as I can remember, I have had a passion for understanding people and seeing the beauty in all things."

A Charlottesville resident for more than a decade, she spends her days documenting people, creating in the kitchen, working on an old house, and living a joy-filled life with her husband, Matt, two young sons, Albert and Cramer, and their two dogs. Sarah has run her own business documenting people professionally for the past twelve years, and her work has taken her around the world, documenting weddings all over the country, art projects in the Midwest, and celebrity chefs right here in Charlottesville. Her images portray a perfectly honest reflection of you, the people you love, and the moment you're in. She lives to tell stories. In 2015, Sarah built a new photography studio, custom-designed for her unique natural light photography.

Please visit her website sarahcramershields.com to see her work and learn more.

About Kristin

Col '14

Kristin Perry is the Production Manager at Mascot Books and served as the project manager for Hoos in the Kitchen. *As a graduate of the University of Virginia, working on a UVA cookbook was a dream come true and showed her how much better she could have eaten throughout college.*

While at UVA, she enjoyed frequenting the Corner, spending time on the Lawn, and studying in the Music Library. After earning degrees in English and psychology, Kristin found her calling in helping authors see their book ideas come to life. She now lives in Fairfax, Virginia, and loves to visit her other home in Charlottesville every chance she gets.

Gallatin Canyon

Laura Brown, representing the Local Food Hub

MS Events provided all
tablescape decor

Flowers provided by Nature Composed

Tablescape designed by Kelsey Harrell of The Catering Outfit

www.mascotbooks.com

Hoos in the Kitchen

Second Printing

For more information, please contact:

Mascot Books

620 Herndon Parkway #320

Herndon, VA 20170

info@mascotbooks.com

CPSIA Code: PRTWP0318B

ISBN-13: 978-1-63177-639-7

Printed in Malaysia